Public Relations Campaigns and Portfolio Building

Gemma R. Puglisi, M.A.

American University

Allyn & Bacon

Boston   Columbus   Indianapolis   New York   San Francisco   Upper Saddle River
Amsterdam   Cape Town   Dubai   London   Madrid   Milan   Munich   Paris   Montreal   Toronto
Delhi   Mexico City   Sao Paulo   Sydney   Hong Kong   Seoul   Singapore   Taipei   Tokyo

3 4 5 6 7 8 9 10—V036 —14 13 12 11

Allyn & Bacon
is an imprint of

www.pearsonhighered.com   ISBN-10: 0-205-82410-2
                           ISBN-13: 978-0-205-82410-6

Contents

Introduction

After having spent many years in a network newsroom during the 1980s and early 1990s, I found myself entering a new and quite different field: public relations. It was quite a departure for me. At that time, many people asked why I was going to the "dark side" like Darth Vader in *Star Wars*. But was it really that? As I continued my career working as a public relations practitioner in both the business sector and PR firms, I realized that my role was as an advocate—standing for something that was important and being truthful about it.

As our field has evolved, there is no question that without public relations, no business, organization, company, political figure or celebrity could survive. Thus began my passion for the field.

As I made the transition from the office to the classroom, I realized that there was no true textbook or guide to help students understand the essentials of what makes the perfect portfolio.

The portfolio class is to me, the final "hurrah" before you enter the real world. And to me, this class should encompass all that you have learned and more. We are in a field that is constantly changing. Each day we see these changes.

My hope is that this book provides you with a framework of how to put together the perfect portfolio for your first real job in the public relations field. It is also a guide or a map, if you will, of what a portfolio class could entail to help you reach your full potential. At the same time, may it be an inspiration on how to help others in the community, and leave a legacy of your work and your passion. Godspeed.

Gemma Puglisi

Acknowledgments

There are so many people I would like to thank for their help in putting this manual together.

First, my sincere thanks to Jeanne Zalesky with the Pearson Education Group, who agreed that there was a need for a Portfolio guidebook for students. Thanks, Jeanne. Special thanks to Jerry Higgins, also with Pearson, who never stopped encouraging me with the idea and the book. Jerry, you are the best! My deepest thanks to the extraordinary work and time the project manager, Anne Ricigliano, spent with me on the final stages of the book, and to the wonderful formatter, Rocky Buckley at Black Diamond Graphics, who put in all the finishing touches. Anne and Rocky, thank you for your incredible guidance and patience. I would also like to thank the others who gave me permission to reference their books with Pearson and Thomson Wadsworth, respectively, and these include my colleagues Dennis Wilcox, Professor Emeritus, San Jose State University, and Barbara Diggs Brown, Professor Emeritus, American University.

I would also like to specifically acknowledge and profusely thank Perez Hilton for the mention of his site, www.perezhilton.com; as well as everyone with Lifetime Entertainment Services LLC and "Project Runway," including Katherine A. Pack; William Swann with the Weinstein Company; hosts Tim Gunn and Heidi Klum; and Season 6 winner Irina Shabeyeva. Your reference in the book is inspiring for future students to see that there are no limits to what they can achieve.

Thanks to the other various organizations that we have had the honor of working with over the past several years during my time here as a professor at American University. You have my appreciation and gratitude for your support and constant encouragement to the students. They include: Elizabeth Gore, Executive Director of

Global Partnerships and Nothing but Nets for the United Nations Foundation; Rob Rutland-Brown, Executive Director of Just Neighbors—Immigration Legal Services; Reem Azoury, owner of the "Figs Fine Foods" café in Georgetown; the folks at Neediest Kids including Lynne Filderman, Executive Director; Jane E. Cohen, President; and Lynne Downer, Manager, Operations & Administration; John and Joyce Wanda, co-founders, Arlington Academy of Hope; Jennifer Paul, former Executive Director, Arlington Academy of Hope; Patricia Wudel, Executive Director of Joseph's House; Dr. David Hilfiker, founder of Joseph's House; and last but certainly not least, my colleagues at American University's Kennedy Political Union, Will Hubbard and Matthew Swibel. I would also like to thank another colleague at American, Professor Rick Rockwell, whose journalism students worked on a beautiful documentary about men and women returning from the war in the "Homefront" project and the university faculty publication, *American Today*. Special thanks to producer Janet Terry and correspondent Andrea Roane with WUSA-TV, Channel 9 for usage of a photo from a video clip; Franco Nuschese for actually participating in the first real-world portfolio several years ago for his restaurant, Sette Bello in Clarendon, Virginia; and American University Professor and colleague, Dr. Jeffrey Schaler, who teaches Justice, Law and Society. Thank you to the wonderful Kristi Plahn-Gjersvold at American for always being there to help in every way. Also special thanks to an extraordinary young man and friend, Pete Muntean, who worked graciously with the students following his mom's tragic death in an air show in the fall of 2007. My thanks to Michele Danoff and Graphics Design for usage of a photo of Pete's mom, Nancy Lynn, taken several years before her death. I would also like to recognize the extraordinary people with the Wounded Warrior Regiment, including Colonel Gregory A. Boyle and Captain Leticia Reyes for working with my graduate students on a groundbreaking project and the first year celebration of the organization.

I would like to stress that, as a professor, I did my best to acknowledge the work of each individual student. My sincerest apologies to those whose assignments I may have unintentionally left out from this book. Since I have taught this class for so many years, it is impossible for me to keep track of all specific assignments and works by each student. I appreciate your understanding.

Finally, I would like to thank my fabulous researcher, Allison Lane, for her time, insight, and guidance on every aspect of this manual. You are wonderful.

I would also like to acknowledge my incredible family for their constant love and support in all I do inside and outside the classroom: my dear and wonderful sisters, Dr. Angela Puglisi and Beatrice Tierney; my beautiful nieces Lauren Hraba and Monica Tierney; my incredible brother in-law, John Tierney, Jr.; and my dashing and fabulous nephews John Tierney, III, and Michael Hraba!

And in memory of my extraordinary parents, Vittorio and Carmela Puglisi, whose passion for education and the goodness in life continues to inspire me.

I dedicate this book to all my Portfolio students—for making me not only a better teacher, but a better human being.

Heather Abrams	Mary Campbell	Erin Fagan
Shermeen Ahmad	Natasha Carlos	Erin Fechko
Teressa Alberts	Tiffany Carter	Jessie Ferguson
Heather Albarazi	Raiza Castro	Megan Fillebrown
Michael Alderfer	Jacqueline Chamberlain	Lauren Fox
Ninnar Alqames	Cathleen Chandler	Leah Fulner
Artemis Antippas	Randar Chappin	Amanda Fulton
Marisa Applestein	Dolores Chavez	Erin Galgay
Jennifer Arosemena	Toniann Chetta	Lisa Galik
	Amy Chin	Isel Galvan
Abigail Baram	Mari Chin	Keri Garman
Laura Barnes	Marissa Chmiola	Alyssa Geisler
Celia Barreda	Natalie Collier	Lara Goldstein
Kelly Barrett	Bethany Corey	Emily Golomb
Kimberly Beauman	Jennifer Crawford	Andrew Gordon
Stephanie Beauparlant		Katie Gibbs
Andrea Becker	Mara Da Silva	Caitlin Green
Samya Behary	Mark DeSantis	Arielle Greenberg
Carolyn Benton	Kaitlin Detroia	Elyse Greenberg
Tiffany Bertrand	Paula Dibley	Jacqueline Grosser
Daniel Bleier	Jessica Dirocco	Lisa Gruber
Sarah Boison	Molly Doyle	
Jennifer Bonhomme	Vandana Duggal	Yoon Hwa Han
Margaret Brink	Louelin Dwyer	Jacob Hanna
Lindsey Brothers		Raymond Hauserman
Tamara Brown	Hannah Ellsworth	Carleen Hawthorne
Kimberly Bryden	Tessie Epstein	Lindsay Hayek
Arielle Burlett		Caroline Helfman
Katherine Byrne		Marisa Herbert

Amanda Hesse

Mollie Jo Holman

Nicole Howard

Nicole Hunter

Lauren Isen

Mary Jackson

Kaitlin Jacobi

Brittany Johnson

Banafsaj Kanaan

Kadia Kane

Tracy Kania

Nikoleta Keeney

Emily Kline

Daryn Koo

Kate Kovarovic

Maile Krauss

Jessica Krupke

Karie Kvandal

Anthony Lafauce

Amanda Lamb

Benjamin Lamson

Laura Landrau

Daniel Lanini

Tammy Lee

Robin Levine

Catherine Licht

David Lieberson

Ann Liu

Salome Limbaro

Michael Lock

Robert MacDonald

Taylor Mach

Arzu Maliki

Hope Mandel

Lauren Marchi

Maggie McGrath

Lorna Middlebrough

Hillary Molare

Sara Nevius

Deanna Niles

Anna Nix

Jennifer O'Holla

Halley Ofner

Hannah Oh

Amanda Ongirski

Jung Park

Remy Pascale

Jason Paul

Lucas Pierce

Maria Piessis

Dex Polizzi

Alyssa Pridgen

Raven Radley

Correy Robertson

Shayli Roiz

Sara Rojas

Amanda Rollins

Nasser Romaithy

Alyssa Romano

Saverio Romeo

Scott Rosania

Adam Rosenblatt

Anna Rubin

Mary Rucker

Notoya Russell

Alexandra Salama

Molly Sauer

April Saylor

Brian Schachter

Gema Schaerer

Hilary Schlimbach

Meredith Schlosser

Adam Schroeder

Dawn Selak

Hallie Seltzer

Bettina Sferrino

Paul Sideris

Allison Smith

Rebecca Smith

Aimee Solomon

Jaymee Soojian

Athelstan Spilhaus

Lauren Spitzer

Jeffra Stafford

Jessica Stark

Brendan Steidle

Mark Stern

Alyssa Stieglitz

Logan Striebel

Sabrina Sussman

Eric Sveum

Alison Swift

Marivic Tagala

Marissa Tasho

McKenna Taylor

Peter Thai

Michaela Thayer

Ryan Tilden

Cheryl Tilghman

Margaret Tolly

Amy Tomlinson

Ann Marie Tropiano

Natalie Veliz

Cristina Villaraos

Cosima Wadhwa

Caitlin Ward

Jessica Warren

Leslie Wasserman

Kaitlin Wiley

Rachelle Wilson

Eleanor Willard

Kaysha Williams

Elizabeth Wineriter

Lena Winkler

Mayu Yamamoto

Christine Young

Meghan Young

Meghan Zichelli

1

Back to Basics

These are changing times, and although that may sound like a cliché, it is true. But if there is one constant, it is building a solid foundation to tackle the field of public relations. No matter what new technologies come our way, we must be aware of the basics. Those basics include understanding what a client wants, needs, and must have to survive. And to be truly successful, you must do what the father of public relations, Edward L. Bernays, stressed: "The [pr] practitioner must work hard, but with ability and enthusiasm. He can make his road lead to wherever he will."[1]

Another important leader in the field was Arthur W. Page, "a longtime vice president for public relations at AT&T, and often regarded as the founder of the modern practice of corporate public relations." Page believed in the integrity of our field and came up with his own set of principles that a practitioner should remember.[2] These seven principles include:

- Tell the truth

- Prove it with action

- Listen to the customer

- Manage for tomorrow

---

[1] Larson, K.A. (1978) *Public Relations, the Edward L. Bernayses, and the American Scene: A Bibliography*. Boston: F.W. Faxon Company, Inc., p. 4.
[2] Arthur W. Page Society (2010). *Seven Proven Principles That Guide Our Actions and Behaviors*. Retrieved from www.awpagesociety.com.

- Conduct public relations as if the whole company depends on it

- Realize a company's true character is expressed by its people

- Remain calm, patient, and good-humored

Keeping in mind these two brilliant PR leaders, you should be in good shape to forge ahead.

Forging ahead means knowing whom your client is, what they want, and what they need. You must do your homework...you must **research, research, research.**

Today we are lucky to have the internet, which provides so much information. But you must do your homework. What is the company's *message?* Is it conveyed easily in all this research? Talk to your colleagues, your friends, and your family. Do they know the company or organization? What is their opinion of the organization? Comb those local newspapers, newsletters, websites, and community leaflets. Social media such as Facebook, Twitter, blogs, and YouTube, just to name a few, are instrumental today. Without a doubt, one reason why Barack Hussein Obama won the presidency, experts say, is because of the power of social media.

Yes, it's true the internet is a goldmine on so many levels. However, communities still have their own means of communication via leaflets, fliers, and quarter sheets. (We see them on our campuses.) Remember the impact Thomas Paine's *Common Sense*[3] had on the beginnings of our country's independence in 1776. More than 120,000 copies were sold in three months during that period. Now that may be a small figure by today's standards, but in 1776, reaching that number in a short amount of time was powerful, profound, and led to the formation of our government.

Once you have done a thorough amount of research, you are ready to begin the planning of the program. What are the elements of a PR plan?[4] Here they are, but with some modification for your Portfolio class:

---

[3] Wilcox, Dennis L., Cameron, Glen T., Ault, Phillip H., and Agee, Warren K. *Public Relations: Strategies and Tactics*, 9th Edition. Boston: Pearson Education, Inc., 2003, p. 41.
[4] Ibid.

- **Situation**—Does the client have to "overcome" a problem or situation? Are you helping them with just one project or event? Do they need to reinforce their reputation or do they need public support?

- **Objectives**—What is realistic to achieve? Is the objective motivational or informational?

- **Audience**—Is there a specific audience? Can you broaden that audience? Is there a global audience? How can you take it one step beyond the obvious?

- **Strategy**—The "broad statement" describing how you will achieve the objectives. The strategy provides the guidelines and key message themes for the overall program.

- **Tactics**—The "nuts-and-bolts" of your plan. Take the "a-c-t" in Tactics and ask yourself, "What activities will I plan to reach my goals?"

- **Calendar-Timetable**—Our semester lasts about 15 weeks. How long is your semester or class? What are you able to achieve in those weeks? Also, what will you leave the organization/client with after you are finished? Is there a timetable to help them down the road?

- **Budget**—Do you have one? Does your client have a small budget for you? Or is there none? What do you have to work with?

- **Evaluation**—Were you successful? Did you reach your audience(s)? Did you get the media's attention? Did you connect with others via social networking? Was your event successful?

You must remember those elements like riding a bike. Even as a professor, I study these elements with each case to make certain that everything has been taken into consideration. You must not forget them!

I emphasize understanding the power of research and knowing your eight elements of a PR plan before you walk into your first

PR Portfolio class. Some of you will be aware of what's ahead by the syllabi your professors provide online prior to your first class. Generally for me, I do not post the syllabi online. Reason: I like to surprise my students on the first day of class by telling them the name of the client. By the second class, the students are asked to do research on the client and prepare questions. That second class is when the students actually meet the client and hear of their needs and their goals. The approach is to make this process as realistic as possible—as you would in any meeting with a prospective client.

How to Find the Perfect Client...or How They Find You

Whether you are a student at a community college, a private institution, a big university, or a small liberal arts college, you will find a client. Believe me! The state of the economy in 2008 and 2009 changed the world for many nonprofits, small businesses, and organizations. In 2008, of the nearly 1 million nonprofits up and running, the prediction was that over 100,000 would fail over the coming six months.[1] Remember these organizations are in such need of help that they welcome the ideas and the brilliancy of students. And they are eternally grateful. You will also leave your mark on their lives and make a difference.

How do you find clients no matter where you are?

- **Newspapers and magazines**—Some of the best classes have evolved from print articles or feature stories about small businesses or nonprofits. That is why we still need these means of communication.

- **Community groups**—Be proactive. Find out about the different groups and organizations in your community. If you

---

[1] Light, P. C. (2008, November 28). "Obama Must Mobilize Supporters to Help Nonprofits." In www.washingtonpost.com. Retrieved from www.washingtonpost.com.

are in a city that has mass transportation, look around you. Look at some of the ads posted. They may spark some ideas about a group or organization.

- **Babysitting**—Some students babysit in their areas to make a living. Many of the families they babysit for belong to organizations or clubs. Find out if there are any you can help.

- **Social networking**—Check Facebook, MySpace, LinkedIn, and other sites. Find out what your classmates and colleagues are working on. It could open up a new world for you in terms of helping an organization.

- **What clubs, sororities, and fraternities are on campus?** Could you take one of their charities or organizations they believe in and help them for 15 weeks?

- **National organizations**—Check to see if there are local chapters of national organizations and charities in your area. They likely work with their national chapters and your work may be instrumental in their upcoming campaigns.

- **Small businesses**—Are there small businesses that need your support to survive in your community? Small businesses help economic growth, provide jobs, and make a difference in communities. Can you help a startup?

- **Human rights**—Is there any organization or institution that helps human rights? Does it play a role in gender issues, racial issues, equality, or the rights of individuals? These could be monumental for your class.

- **Alumni**—Many students come to me after graduation after they have found employment. Some of the companies they work for are in need of help on projects, etc. Keep in contact with those friends or former students.

- **Celebrities**—I find that many students follow celebrities and what they do. Is there a charity or organization that a celebrity believes in that you think you can help in your area? Or can you contact that celebrity about the work that you are doing for their support? (Example: See Photo 2.1).

PHOTO 2.1. Placement of Just Neighbors on the Perez Hilton website. Students Amanda Fulton and Jackie Grosser secured this mention for the client, Just Neighbors. (*Source*: http://perezhilton.com//2010-02-09-a-worthwhile-cause-509)

Students in one of the classes contacted celebrity blogger Perez Hilton, who recognizes "worthwhile causes" on his website. Long after the students graduated, Perez posted information on his site (www.perezhilton.com) about "Just Neighbors," an organization that provides legal immigration services to low-income immigrants and refugees. What a tribute to the students! The legacy continues for them.

- **Other departments in your school**—You may be a student in the Communications department, but you may have colleagues that are studying justice, business, or international service. Do you have several sports teams on campus that desperately need publicity? Tap into these resources. Working together with other units could be invaluable—so don't underestimate the power of numbers.

Once you have established yourself, you will find that organizations will come to you and welcome your talents!

3

Strategy

What are the client's needs and how can you as a class work on the plan? As we discussed in the very first chapter, "Back to Basics," you must look at all of the elements in the plan:

- Situation
- Objectives
- Audience
- Strategy
- Tactics
- Calendar
- Timetable
- Budget
- Evaluation

It is important to identify the client's objective. Is it motivational? Is it informational? Is it both? What is the realistic goal and can you reach it in one semester? If you look at the reality, most public relations firms generally have a few people working with a client. This could be on a month-to-month basis. It could be less than a month. It could also be from project-to-project. There is a luxury of having fifteen weeks to achieve goals. And having 20 students or more working for your organization is the icing on the cake. With that said, the stakes are higher. You want to show your client that you did everything you possibly could to deliver the goods. The goods? Media, more visibility, more people who know about their message, and perhaps more contributions.

So once that plan is in place, you need to communicate the **message**. What is that message? That is important. Hopefully, most clients already have that message developed, but since you are their practitioner, you could elaborate on it or reinforce it. There are so many textbooks that describe the theory of "messaging," but perhaps the simplest and best definition is the one in Webster's dictionary: "an underlying theme or idea."[1] This is the dictionary I've kept since my college years, and even in the day of technology, I still keep it by my desk for old times' sake. Thus, your role is to get this "theme" or "idea" out to the audience. Who is your audience?

---

[1] *Webster's New Collegiate Dictionary.* (1973) Springfield, Massachusetts: G & C Merriam Company, p. 715.

4

Working with
the Client

You now have your client. You now have the plan in place. "Let the games begin." There are a few things you must keep in mind. You would think that working for someone pro bono would be a piece of cake. Sadly, it is not. In my experience, working with clients can be wonderful, but at times, challenging. It is vital that when you pick a client, you make certain that you set the tone for how you want to communicate with them during the project.

After all, we are in the communications business. Let me clarify. If you are in a big class and many of you are working with the client, you should establish team leaders. (More information on teams in Chapter 5.) You don't want 15 people or 20 people calling or e-mailing your client.

Designate team leaders and determine how the client wants to be contacted. Do they prefer e-mail or an occasional call? Again, the impact of the internet is remarkable, but my students also communicate by picking up the phone often to make certain that everyone is on the same page and there is a mutual understanding of the goals and expectations. If students send e-mails and there is no response, the phone calls begin. That kind of communication is essential. How often does the client want to be contacted? Should you send a weekly report to keep them up-to-date? If you are on spring or fall break, how do they contact you? These are all-important questions and should be ironed out at the very beginning of the class. Once you've established all this, the class should work smoothly.

You should also make certain that there is another person other than your main contact at the organization in the event of an emergency. In this economic climate, you don't know what organizations are going through, and having two contacts is essential to help things run seamlessly.

Thirdly, this is **not** an internship. Repeat. **Not** an internship. You as students should set the tone. If you get the sense from the beginning that the client doesn't understand this, get another client. I have found this to be true in cases where students want to find the client on their own. Things go well in the beginning, but then suddenly the client doesn't react, doesn't get back to the students, and everything is in limbo. Sadly, this is an awful business practice, and the sense is that some of these clients believe the relationship is an internship. *Educating a client is essential.* But don't hesitate to end the relationship and find another client who would appreciate your hard work and talents.

There could be other challenges as well. Some clients, and not all, may look at you as students and not understand the ideas and suggestions you offer. A few may not want to make the changes you recommend. And some of you may want to tell them the truth but not know how. That is our role as PR practitioners. We are counselors as well, and our work makes a difference in the community and the world. Remember Bernays' words in *Crystallizing Public Opinion:* "The public relations consultant is ideally a constructive force in the community. The results of his work are often accelerated in matters of value and importance to the social, economic, or political life of the community."[1] Again, here is a guideline when working with your clients:

---

[1] Bernays, E. L. (1923). *Crystallizing Public Opinion.* New York: Liverlight Publishing Corporation, p. 57.

FEATURE BOX: PUGLISI'S GUIDELINES

1. Set the tone at the beginning—identify method/time of communicating.

2. Make certain there is a second contact in the event of emergencies.

3. Limit the number of people contacting your client.

4. Be assertive.

5. Be professional and honest.

6. Know your place and be respectful.

7. Stand your ground. If there are challenges, communicate with them and work on how to improve the relationship.

8. Don't be afraid to contact your professor to intervene at any point should there be serious problems with the client.

9. Be proud of your work.

10. Maintain a good relationship with the client even after graduating.

The other important issue in all this is a budget. Do you have any funds at all given to you by the client? Is there any budget allotted to you by your department or university? Is there a business or organization in your community that values your work as students and has given you a small grant to work with? These are all-important and must be determined at the very beginning.

5

Teamwork

Part of your PR plan is deciding how you want to work with the client, as mentioned earlier. In a classroom situation and in real life, there are often teams that work together to get the job done. It depends on the number of students in the class—and if you want teams. There are pros and cons of working together as a team in schools, but it is an important function, and learning to collaborate successfully is what life is about. Thus, working on an actual PR plan with team members is essential.

To help navigate through all this, I will use an example from one of my classes. Our client was the United Nations Foundation and their *Nothing But Nets* campaign. It was such a worthwhile project, and they have done extraordinary work to help prevent the spread of malaria in Africa. Just a brief history:

"In 2006, the United Nations Foundation created *Nothing But Nets*, a global, grassroots campaign to save lives by delivering long-lasting insecticide-treated bed nets to communities in Africa."[1] These bed nets are considered one of the most effective ways to prevent malaria. They cost $10 and making this donation is "sending a net and saving a life." According to the UN Foundation, every year between "300–500 million people become infected with malaria." One million die from the infection, and tragically, children are the biggest victims. The big, compelling message that the

---

[1] *Nothing But Nets* (2009). Retrieved on May 4, 2010 from www.nothingbutnets.net/about-the-campaign.

students learned was: "Every 30 seconds a child dies from malaria." A powerful message that tells the story.

The project came to us from one of my former students, Kate Kovarovic. Kate was one of those extraordinary students that you never forget, so when she approached me about the project, it was a done deal. The first day of class, students heard about the client and what the organization does. In the second class, the students met the client and asked questions. Their responsibility was to **research, research, research**. They had to learn as much about the client as possible. As the students talked to the client, they began to see the shape of their plan. What did the client want from college students? What was their hope? How do they get the message across to other college students? And what legacy would they leave? The bottom line: The client wanted more college students involved in the campaign. It was up to the class to determine how to achieve this. Thus began the shaping of the teams.

In the third class, students began the discussion on how to work with the client and what teams could be formed.

The result: **five teams**. I also asked the students to come up with their own names for the teams. (See **Feature Box: Team Names** on the facing page.)

Once the teams were established, the PR plan was ready to take shape. These teams knew what their responsibilities were, how to work with one another, and how to execute the plan. Yes, it's true that not all members of a team work together, but it is a learning experience and part of life. The more you realize what your role is and what challenges you face, the better you will be at handling pressures and getting the work done.

FEATURE BOX: TEAM NAMES

TEAM 1: TEAM T4

Involved creating marketing tools. The four represented the four students.

TEAM 2: BGs

These students worked on a couple of events for college students in the area to attend. The name of the group represented the initials of the students in the group.

TEAM 3: TEAM CAMPERS

These students worked on events strictly on campus to raise money for the organization. Thus the name "Campers."

TEAM 4: TEAM SUV

These students worked on securing overall media. Again, the name represented the students' initials.

TEAM 5: BMW

These students worked solely on activities for "Malaria Awareness Week" activities on campus. That took place the last week of April. Again, the team name represented the students' initials.

MEDIA ADVISORY

<u>For Immediate Release</u>

Date you are sending release. (Ex. Feb. 8, 2008)

Main Headline Focused on Biggest Newsworthy Item
Subtitle if desired

WHAT: Include a brief description of your event.

WHO: List names of sponsors and/or public figures who will attend your event. (Ex. Name, *Title*)

WHEN: Date of event and time. Include a schedule if there are multiple events.

WHERE: Location
           Street Address
           City, State   Zip

           Parking information:

WHY: Between 300 - 500 million people become infected with malaria each year and one million people die from the disease. The majority of those infected are children under the age of five. Fortunately, malaria is a preventable disease. Now, the [STUDENT ORGANIZATION] at [UNIVERSITY NAME] is joining Nothing *But Nets* in the fight against malaria.

About *Nothing But Nets*

Nothing But Nets is a global, grassroots campaign to save lives by preventing malaria, a leading killer of children in Africa. Inspired by former *Sports Illustrated* columnist Rick Reilly, tens of thousands of people have joined the Campaign that was created by the United Nations Foundation in 2006. Founding campaign partners include the National Basketball Association's NBA Cares, The People of the United Methodist Church, and *Sports Illustrated*. It only costs $10 to provide an insecticide-treated bed net that can prevent this deadly disease. Visit www.NothingButNets.net to send a net and save a life.

CONTACT: [CONTACT NAME, TITLE]
           [PHONE NUMBER]
           [EMAIL ADDRESS].

\#\#\#

TRY TO LIMIT MEDIA ADVISORY TO ONE PAGE

Photo 6.2. Example of template created by student Marissa Chmiola for other universities and colleges to use for *Nothing But Nets* campaign.

NothingButNets.net

NEWS RELEASE

Date of distribution
FOR IMMEDIATE RELEASE

Contact Information:
[Name, Title]
[Office: (###) ###-####]
[Fax: (###) ###-###]
[Email:]

<u>**HEADLINE: Uppercase letters, bold and underlined; states summary of news**</u>
SUBHEAD: Upper- and lowercase letters, bold and italicized. Supplements news headline and does not paraphrase

[DATELINE: WASHINGTON, DC] – On [DATE OF EVENT], [NAME OF COLLEGE/UNIVERSITY OR COLLEGE ORGANIZATION] will be hosting [EVENT]. The students of [NAME OF COLLEGE/UNIVERSITY OR COLLEGE ORGANIZATION] are doing their part to support *Nothing But Nets,* a campaign whose mission is to save a life one net at a time.

Every 30 seconds a child dies from malaria and every day 25 million pregnant African American women risk severe illness and harm to their unborn children from a malaria infection. *Nothing But Nets* is a global, grassroots campaign that saves lives by delivering long-lasting insecticide-treated nets to prevent malaria. Their message is simple: Malaria kills. Nets save lives. Send a net. Save a life. [NAME OF COLLEGE/UNIVERSITY] students are saving lives one net at a time by getting their college peers and community involved in this worthy campaign.

[DESCRIBE EVENT. POINT OUT SPECIAL ACTIVITIES, GUEST SPEAKERS, FOOD, AND DONATION INFORMATION].

[TWO OR MORE QUOTATIONS FROM RELEVANT SOURCES SUCH AS LEAD ORGANIZER, STUDENTS ON CAMPUS OR A QUOTE FROM THE COLLEGE/UNIVERSITY PRESIDENT].

Photo 6.3. Press Release/News Release—Students created a template for other universities to use. This can guide you for your own campaigns.

PAGE 2 OF 2

[BOILERPLATE: SUMMARIZE THE PHILOSPHY, GOALS, AND PURPOSE OF YOUR

ORGANIZATION AND/OR COLLEGE/UNIVERSITY. IT SHOULD APPEAR JUST BEFORE THE

END OF THE NEWS RELEASE].

-###-

About *Nothing But Nets*
Nothing But Nets is a global, grassroots campaign to save lives by preventing malaria, a leading killer of children in Africa. Inspired by former *Sports Illustrated* columnist Rick Reilly, tens of thousands of people have joined the Campaign that was created by the United Nations Foundation in 2006. Founding campaign partners include the National Basketball Association's NBA Cares, The People of the United Methodist Church, and *Sports Illustrated*. It only costs $10 to provide an insecticide-treated bed net that can prevent this deadly disease. Visit www.NothingButNets.net to send a net and save a life.

CONTACT: [CONTACT NAME, TITLE]
             [PHONE NUMBER]
             [EMAIL ADDRESS].

Photo 6.3.1. Press Release/News Release, continued.

You, as a student, can certainly send these releases to your local media, your school paper, and your school radio and television stations to inform them of the project. Remember that your release should be in the "inverted pyramid style," with the most important or interesting information conveyed first, followed by information that is increasingly less important.[1] (See Photos 6.3 and 6.3.1.)

- **Pitch Letter**—A letter to individual members of the media asking them to do a one-on-one interview with a spokesperson, celebrity, CEO, or member of an organization about a newsworthy event. Can also be used to request that the media cover the story. (See Photo 6.4.)

[1] Diggs-Brown, B. (2007) *The PR Style Guide: Formats for Public Relations Practice*, 2nd Edition. California: Thomson Wadsworth, p. 136.

Malaria kills. Send a net. Save a life.

[Date. (Ex. Feb. 7, 2008)]

[Reporter's Name]
[Title]
[Media Outlet]
[Street Address]
[City, State. Zipcode]

Dear Mr./Ms. [Last Name]:

I am writing to suggest a story on [ORGANIZATION NAME]'s partnership with *Nothing But Nets* to engage [UNIVERSITY NAME] students in the fight against malaria.

[ORGANIZATION NAME] at [UNIVERSITY NAME] will be hosting a [EVENT TYPE] on [DATE] to raise money for the distribution of insecticide-treated net used to prevent malaria. [INCLUDE 1 – 2 SENTENCES DESCRIBING EVENT.]

All of the money raised during this event will be donated to *Nothing But Nets*. Founded in 2006 by the United Nations Foundation, *Nothing But Nets* is a global, grassroots campaign to save lives by delivering insecticide-treated nets to communities in Africa. To date, the campaign has engaged over 60,000 individuals, raised more than $18 million and distributed over 730,000 nets.

"[ORGANIZATION NAME] is excited to be working with *Nothing But Nets* to raise money at [UNIVERSITY NAME] for the distribution of mosquito nets," said [ORGANIZATION NAME] president [PRESIDENT'S NAME]. "One million people die each year from malaria, but it's a preventable disease. It only takes $10 to buy a net and save a life. We are happy we can do our part in the fight against malaria."

We hope your readers will be inspired by this story of university students who are actively engaged in the fight against malaria. For more information about our organization and event you can contact me at [XXX-XXX-XXXX] or at [EMAIL ADDRESS]. [ORGANIZATION NAME] president [PRESIDENT'S NAME] can be reached at [XXX-XXX-XXXX] or at [EMAIL ADDRESS]. To learn more about *Nothing But Nets*, log on to **NothingButNets.net**. Thank you for your time.

Sincerely,

[COMMUNICATION COORDINATOR/CONTACT NAME]
[TITLE WITHIN ORGANIZATION]

***NOTE: KEEP LETTER TO ONE PAGE IN LENGTH. ADJUST MARGINS OR EDIT IF NECESSARY ***

Photo 6.4. Pitch Letter—Again, a template to be used for possible media placements.

- **Quarter Sheets**—Sheets that are a quarter of a page that can be distributed to your organizations, campuses, and metro/subway stops to inform people about an event. (See Photos 6.5 and 6.5.1.)

Photo 6.5. Quarter Sheets—These quarter sheets are designed to be individual flyers to promote your events. Students can distribute them throughout the campus.

Photo 6.5.1. Quarter Sheets, continued.

- **Brochure**—Generally a sheet of paper that is folded into two sections. Could also include a bigger size sheet that is divided into three sections. These tools are generally colorful and include photos and artwork about an organization and what it does. Brochures generally include statistics about the organization. (See Photo 6.6.)

Photo 6.6. Brochure—Example of one side of a tri-fold brochure. Designed by student Emily Golomb; photo by Kike Arnal.

- **Newsletter**—A means of internal and external communication available to an organization.[2] Features news about the organization and what it does, including events, people in the news, and future items.

- **Media List**—This is a compilation of all the media outlets that you may want to target for your client and their campaign. Now many clients may have this, but I have found that as students, you are creative and can find other media to get the message across. (In the case with *Nothing But Nets*, students also included D.C.-based blogs, newspapers, as well as bridal, sports, and travel magazines. The reason: We had learned that some couples asked for donations in lieu of gifts for their weddings. Also, several "net" organizations were very supportive of the organization, including the National Basketball Association (NBA) and the Women's National Basketball Association (WNBA), and we wanted to target sports enthusiasts who could potentially support the organization. And finally, people who travel to other parts of the world need to know about malaria and how to prevent it.)

- **Invitations**—These can range from being simple to elaborate, but it is essentially a card or note expressing your desire for someone to attend an event. It is a formal method of inviting individuals. (See Photos 6.7 and 6.7.1.)

---

[2] Diggs-Brown, B. (2007) *The PR Style Guide: Formats for Public Relations Practice*, 2nd Edition. California: Thomson Wadsworth, p. 111.

*In celebration of our partnership
with the Wounded Warrior Regiment*

THE AU SCHOOL OF COMMUNICATION
GRADUATE PRACTICUM CLASS
PRESENTS

BREAKING NEW GROUND

APRIL 22, 2008

Welcome & Introduction

Situation Analysis

Objectives

Looking Forward

Special Presentation

Video Presentation

Closing Remarks

PLEASE JOIN US FOR A RECEPTION
FOLLOWING TODAY'S PRESENTATION.

Photo 6.7. Invitation—Example that can be used to invite your client to the final presentation. Designed by students Denise Lew, Rebecca Potts, and Gail Ziegler.

On behalf of the Spring 2008 Public Communication Graduate Practicum Class under the direction of Professor Gemma Puglisi, we would like to express our sincere gratitude for the opportunity to partner with the United States Marine Corps' Wounded Warrior Regiment.

We would like to recognize the selfless efforts of the Wounded Warrior Regiment, its families and its staff and commend you for your commitment.

We offer this presentation in honor of the sacrifice of our nation's Wounded Warriors. We are grateful for your service and recognize the efforts of Wounded Warriors at home and abroad.

OUR SINCEREST THANKS TO:

Our nation's Wounded Warriors & and their families
Colonel Gregory Boyle
Captain Leticia Reyes
and the staff of the Wounded Warrior Regiment

Photo 6.7.1. Invitation, continued.

- **Fact Sheet**—A one-page background sheet about an event, a product, or even the organization. Such fact sheets may be distributed with a news release or even be part of a media kit.[3] I usually suggest that the fact sheet be in bullet form, though it can be written as an outline. (See Photo 6.8.)

---

[3] Wilcox, D. L. (2009) *Public Relations Writing and Media Techniques*, 6th Edition. Boston: Pearson Education, Inc., p. 141.

fact sheet

AAH in Uganda

Uganda is a landlocked country in East Africa. AAH runs a school, health centers and other programs in Eastern Uganda, about a 7-hour drive from Kampala, the capital city, in a remote, mountainous region near the Kenyan border.

Ugandan Public School System

The Ugandan government offers free primary education to its citizens. However the system is severely under-funded, resulting in:

- Schools with decaying walls or no roofs
- Up to 110 children per classroom
- Unmotivated teachers who do not show up or do not get paid regularly
- Programs without books, pencils, paper or food for students

All students in Uganda must pass the Primary Leaving Exam to continue on to secondary school. Students must pay to attend secondary school and the system has four tiers or divisions; Division One represents top-level boarding schools.

AAH Primary School

- Children are taught a rigorous, traditional curriculum in English, with an emphasis on science, social studies, reading and math
- Children are also taught music, drama, agriculture, domestic care, ecology and handicrafts
- The program encourages participation, debate, critical thinking and self-expression
- AAH provides a midmorning snack, a hot lunch, a uniform, textbooks and school supplies for each student
- Girls are underrepresented in Ugandan public schools, but make up 50% of AAH students and recipients of AAH secondary school scholarships
- AAH requires community service and encourages children and their families to take an active role in the program's growth and development

Academic Results

- For four consecutive years, 100% of AAH students have passed the Primary Leaving Exam
- About 95% of AAH graduates go to top Division One or Division Two secondary schools
- Conversely, less than 14% of Ugandan children who begin primary school advance to secondary school

AAH as an Organization

- AAH is a non-profit 501(c)3 organization, which was founded by John and Joyce Wanda in 2004
- In the U.S., AAH is run almost entirely by volunteers; therefore, nearly 100% of each donation goes to AAH's programs in Uganda
- In Uganda, AAH employs a staff of Ugandan teachers, administrators, and health care workers
- AAH programs in Uganda include the primary school, the secondary scholarship program, two medical clinics, outreach to local village schools and community development initiatives
- AAH strives to serve as a model to lift the standards of education. AAH is exploring building additional schools, partnering with the Ugandan government, adding capacity at local village schools and more to achieve this goal

Donations

Donations of any amount can make a difference and go a long way in Uganda:

$1,000 provides a one-year scholarship to attend secondary school

$500 provides 25 mothers with prenatal and midwife care

$300 sponsors a child's education

$250 covers a teacher's monthly salary

$100 provides malaria treatment to 25 children

$50 feeds lunch to a child for a year

$30 provides textbooks for one child

$25 buys a school uniform

P.O. Box 7694 - Arlington, VA 22207 - 703.201.2483 - www.ArlingtonAcademyofHope.org

Photo 6.8. Fact Sheet—Example highlighting key information about an organization. Includes bullets and items that are succinct and to the point. Created by student Jessica Warren.

- **Backgrounder**—There are several types. One type could focus on a problem and how an organization or a product solved it. Another kind of backgrounder explains how a technology or product has evolved over the years.[4] (See Photo 6.9 for an example.)

---

[4] Wilcox, D. L. (2009) *Public Relations Writing and Media Techniques*, 6th Edition. Boston: Pearson Education, Inc., p. 171.

Malaria kills. Send a net. Save a life.

CAMPAIGN BACKGROUNDER

Nothing But Nets

Nothing But Nets is a global grassroots campaign to save lives by preventing malaria, a leading killer of children in Africa. Inspired by sports columnist Rick Reilly, hundreds of thousands of people have joined the campaign that was created by the United Nations Foundation in 2006. Founding campaign partners include the National Basketball Association's NBA Cares, The people of The United Methodist Church, and *Sports Illustrated*. Other partners include Usher's New Look, vh1, Boy Scouts of America, Major League Soccer's MLS W.O.R.K.S., the National Basketball Association's WNBA Cares, Orkin, Inc., Union For Reform Judaism, the Wasserman Foundation, and Vestergaard-Frandsen.

Malaria Kills

Malaria is preventable, but there are approximately 500 million cases of malaria each year, and nearly 1 million of those infected die from the disease. 90 percent of deaths caused by malaria occur in Africa, where a child dies every 30 seconds from the disease Children who are able to survive malaria are faced with physical and mental impairments, such as poor growth and development. Moreover, every day 25 million pregnant African women risk severe illness and harm to their unborn children from a malaria infection. Malaria contributes to low birth weight among newborn infants, one of the leading risk factors for infant mortality. Malaria incapacitates people and keeps them from working while they recover or take care of sick children. Simply put, malaria keeps countries poor. In addition to the burden on the health system, malaria illness and death cost Africa $12 billion a year in lost productivity.

Send a Net

Every $10 donation to *Nothing But Nets* goes directly toward the purchase, distribution, and education about the proper use of a long-lasting, insecticide-treated bed net. Bed nets work in two ways: they stop mosquitoes from biting during the night and spreading the disease, and the insecticide on the net kills the mosquitoes when they land on it, preventing them from flying on to find their next victim. Bed nets can prevent malaria transmission by 50 percent and up to 90 percent in areas with high-coverage rates.

Save a Life

With your help, we can stop this deadly disease.
Please visit www.NothingButNets.net to send a net and save a life.

NothingButNets.net

Photo 6.9. Backgrounder—A narrative about your organization or client that includes their mission, their history and their achievements.

- **Media Kit**—Though many practitioners use the web to send materials to the press to be more cost-effective, many still use media kits as well. Most media kits consist of a two-pocket folder, containing hard copy news releases, media advisories (alert), feature stories, photographs, slides, backgrounders, biographical sketches, fact sheets, and position papers.[5]
- **Public Service Announcements**—(PSAs) are public communication messages created by or for nonprofit organizations. Executed well, they persuade, inform, or advocate for the public good. The media runs them free of charge on behalf of the organizations.[6]

- **Promotional Items/Giveaways**—These are marketing tools that can include anything from cups, coasters, and pens to t-shirts, bags, etc. (See Photos 6.10 and 6.11 for examples.) They can help elevate your campaign and promote your client's reputation long after you graduate.

---

[5] Diggs-Brown, B. (2007) *The PR Style Guide: Formats for Public Relations Practice*, 2nd Edition. California: Thomson Wadsworth, p. 63.
[6] Ibid., p. 148.

Photo 6.10. Promotional Items—Students created these items for American University's Kennedy Political Union and they were distributed at an event on campus. Created by students Alyssa Pridgen, Brittany Johnson, Amanda Ongirski, Leslie Wasserman and Eric Sveum.

Photo 6.11. Promotional Item—Students also created wristbands for the Arlington Academy of Hope and sold them during the "Recess for Hope" event on campus. Created by student Caitlin Green.

As mentioned, these are just a few of the media tools used in our field and in the classes that may guide you as you work with your clients. Working individually on these tools is obviously essential in honing your skills. You can also vote on your favorite tool as a class. Each of you should be asked to submit your work and omit your name. Then each student votes for his or her favorite one—the winner is the one presented to the client. You can also have the client select their favorite one from the 20 or so students in the class. Competition is good—and it brings out creativity and talent!

7

The Value of Events

If you want to get your message across, there is nothing better than having an event. In your studies you may have learned of the work of Phineas T. Barnum, the great American showman of the 19th century.[1] Barnum was the master of the *pseudo-event*—a major extravaganza that was held to get the media's attention.[2] His work promoting Tom Thumb, a midget that stood just over two feet and weighing 15 pounds, was extraordinary.[3] Thumb was a performer, and Barnum introduced him to society leaders in London and others across the world. Now I'm not suggesting you throw a pseudo-event like Barnum, but I do strongly recommend that you come up with an event (or several) for your client. This is extremely important in reaching your audiences and getting visibility for your client.

Your events can vary and can include any of the following:

- **Panel discussion**—If there is a nonprofit organization involved, you can ask your client to be a panelist and discuss an issue that relates to them. These issues can include homelessness, poverty, educating students in another country, AIDS awareness, globalization, sustainability, etc.

---

[1] Wilcox, Dennis L., Cameron, Glen T., Ault, Phillip H., and Agee, Warren K. *Public Relations: Strategies and Tactics*, 9th Edition. Boston: Pearson Education, Inc., 2003. p. 48.
[2] Ibid., p. 48.
[3] Ibid., p. 48.

Students in one of my classes held a panel discussion for one of our clients, the Arlington Academy of Hope—an organization that works with rural Ugandan communities to build schools and health centers. (See Photo 7.1.)

Tues. March 30 at 8:30pm

American University
Mary Graydon Center
Room 203-205

The School of Communication presents

Sustainable Development:
The Many Facets of Community
Empowerment

Photo 7.1. Program created by student Kelly Barrett.

Photo 7.2 is an example of another event held by students to discuss the issue of homelessness and poverty. Students invited a psychologist and professor from our university, Dr. Jeffrey Schaler, who specializes in human development, along with the founder and executive director of a hospice in Washington, D.C. called "Joseph's House."

JOSEPH'S HOUSE

Homelessness and Healthcare: The Struggle of Living in Poverty

Thursday March 27, 2008
1-2pm
Kay Spirtual Center

Sponsored by,
Senior PR Portfolio Class

Photo 7.2

- **Community event**—Informing your colleagues is a good thing, but letting the community near your college or university know is another. You may be surprised at the responses you'll get from local businesses and community leaders. After all, reaching out to your community about your message is a strong way of helping your organization both now and long after you graduate. Let's discuss one example of how students got a local business to donate food on a specific project. Here's how they did it. (See Photo 7.3.) The class wanted to put together a "penny war" in their dorms. So large plastic bottles were placed on each floor of the dorm and students threw pennies into them. Each penny is worth a point. When someone throws in dimes or coins other than pennies points are deducted. The floor that had the most pennies won. To motivate students, we found a local and popular pizza hangout to donate pies to the winning floor. The manager told us it was the first time our school had approached him for something like this and he was happy to do it. So never underestimate the support of your local community.

Photo 7.3. Designed by student Kimberly Beauman.

- **Campus events**—The ultimate way to inform your school-mates is through your college or university campus. Word spreads quickly and the impact you will have is potentially great. You will find that many organizations want college students involved in some way, so this would be the perfect opportunity for you to leverage your position as a student. Here are some ideas:

  o **Tabling**—Simply renting tables and placing marketing materials and information about your client out for students to take. You can also entice people to stop by your table by having candy or baked goods to give away or sell. (University rules vary on selling food on campus so you may have to check this out before getting started.)

  o Renting an ice cream truck and splitting the proceeds with a vendor.

  o Games and activities on the grounds of your college or university that would attract your classmates to get involved, such as hopscotch, dodgeball, Frisbee, jump rope, etc.

  o Take advantage of holidays. Valentine's Day, St. Patrick's Day, and Halloween are all great days to cele-brate. Think about how can you use these holidays and others to get your client's message across and to get your school involved at the same time. Timing is everything when it comes to events!

- **Off-campus event**—This is perhaps one of the best methods for getting visibility for your client. This type of event would have to include strategies to get your classmates out to attend. It also depends on where you are located. You can work with local businesses to see if they will split some of the proceeds/sales with you. Check local eateries, pizza hang-outs, yogurt shops, bakeries, coffee shops, clothing bou-tiques, just to name a few! (Example: See Photo 7.4). Several years ago, my students held a fundraiser to help Pete Muntean, a young man who lost his mother, Nancy Lynn, in an air show. The students were helping Muntean raise funds for day-to-day expenses as well as to leave a legacy about his mom—one of the few female stunt pilots in the country. One student worked with a local restaurant to organize a fundraiser event. The restaurant agreed to give us about $300 that evening. (Please note: this all varies according to the business. Some agree to a small percentage and others agree based on the amount of people you can bring.)

"Mom, Can you pay for dinner? It's for a good cause!"

Come eat at bd's Mongolian Barbeque to support Pete Muntean and Gemma Puglisi's PR Portfolio class

When: Monday, March 5th
Time: 4-9:30p.m
Where: bd's Mongolian Barbeque
7201 Wisconsin Ave, Bethesda, MD 20814

Photo 7.4. Designed by students Nikoleta Keeney and Nicole Hunter. Photo of Nancy Lynn, courtesy of Michele Danoff, Graphics by Design.

- **Home event**—There are many individuals out there who may want to help with your event/cause, and one way for them to do that is to open their homes to you. This doesn't happen often, but it is worth exploring. A brunch, breakfast, luncheon or evening reception can take place at a home and could involve people in the community and students discussing an important topic/issue that affects your client. Individuals can invite their friends and ask for a donation to attend the party or event. Having you there as a spokesperson for the company could open doors as guests hear about what you do.

Again, these are all examples of how to motivate your community, your classmates, and your school to help your client. There is no question that these events will help you achieve the results you need to gain visibility for the organization.

8

Your Outreach

Obviously, in any campaign your outreach consists of your targeted audience and the media. Many books will teach you to hone in on a specific, "targeted" audience. I will stress the importance of targeting as many people as possible, which will take your campaign from a small level to a higher one. Try to think if there is a "global" audience. Your audience does not have to just involve our country but beyond. Think internationally—and outside the box.

AUDIENCES

Since you are college students, it's only natural that you may want to target your peers and that's essential. Your voices are extremely vital in our world. However, keep in mind other audiences as well. What about your families, your professors/teachers, staffers at your college/university, people in the community, local high school and grade schools, local businesses and local government? All of these audiences are important and they should be examined when discussing strategy for your client. For example, students working with Arlington Academy of Hope wrote to members of Congress for the client and targeted those on the Subcommittee for Africa and Global Health. Students felt it was important for the committee to recognize the work of AAH and the strides they've made with education. (See Photo 8.1).

Students also sent letters to local builders in the area requesting their help with funding a local school in Uganda. The idea was to get builders to "buy a brick" and create a building that would include their support.

Arlington Academy of Hope
P.O Box 7694
Arlington, VA 22207
703.201.2483

Congressman (XXX),

I'm contacting you on behalf of Arlington Academy of Hope (AAH), a volunteer, non-profit organization based in Arlington, VA that helps children in rural Uganda reach their full potential. In light of Monday's devastating landslide in the Ugandan village of Bunametsi, I'm reaching out to you, a member of the (SUBCOMMITTEE), for your support and help in aiding those affected.

I founded AAH in 2004 and opened a model primary school in my home village of Bumwalukani, just three miles from Bunametsi, in order to give children in this area a quality education and a promising future. Beyond that, we offer healthcare and outreach to communities that are in dire need of medical aid. Through this outreach, we hope to serve as a model system for Ugandan education and transform poor villages into self-sustaining communities.

Our school, located in the neighboring village, has seen first hand the devastation that has occurred from the landslide. An estimated 400 people, including 100 school children, were killed in this tragedy, while several of our own students have lost homes and family members as well.

I'm asking for your financial support in order to rebuild not only this community, but also the lives of the thousands of people affected by this disaster, struggling to survive. AAH has established an Emergency Fund to help out the villages buried by the landslide. Not only does this Fund aid in the immediate relief efforts currently underway, but because AAH has a permanent presence in the community, the funds will continue to help for months to come. You may donate by mailing a check to the address above or by giving online through our website.

In addition to this, I ask you to spread the word among your colleagues, who hold the power and the influence to make a difference in these people's lives. As an immigrant from rural Uganda, I've been fortunate enough to have the opportunity to make my own dreams a reality. Now I want to give that opportunity to others, but I need your help to do so.

I would love to find a time in your busy schedule to sit down with you and discuss not only the current relief efforts, but also the work that my organization has been doing in developing these communities for the past six years and our plans to build on this success.

Additional information about AAH is available at www.aahuganda.org but I would be happy to personally answer any questions you may have. Thank you for your time and I look forward to speaking with you.

Sincerely,

John Wanda, Founder
Jwanda2@gmail.com

Photo 8.1

SOCIAL MEDIA

With the advent of the internet, the term "outreach" is now without limits. Many of these boundless outreach possibilities stem from the use of social media. Your generation understands this principle better than anyone. Social media includes the use of websites like Facebook, MySpace, Twitter, YouTube, Foursquare, and many others that are constantly emerging. In all your campaigns, it is essential to use social media to inform your audiences about your client, their events, their mission, and their message. Word travels fast, but it travels faster through social media.

For example, students working with the "Neediest Kids" organization, which helps children in the Washington area, put together a graph to demonstrate the organization's growth of Facebook users. Before the class became involved, Neediest Kids had a handful of Facebook friends. By the end of the semester, the fan base was over 1,000. (See Photo 8.2.)

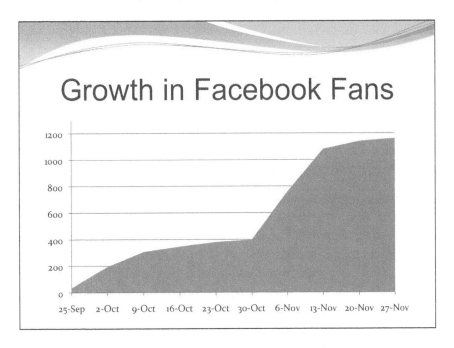

Photo 8.2

Students not only demonstrated the range of their fans, but broke them down according to countries. We had students in the class from the United Emirates and Peru, which helped take their campaign global. (See Photo 8.3.)

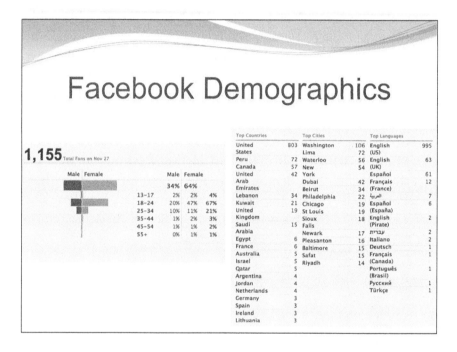

Photo 8.3

Again, this is just a reminder on how your audience base can go way beyond your initial targeted audience.

Perhaps the greatest achievement for the "Neediest Kids" students was their ingenuity. One student who was a fan of the program "Project Runway" on the A&E Lifetime Channel used social media to befriend the last six contestants during the show's sixth season. One of those contestants, Irina Shabayeva, e-mailed him back. (See Photo 8.4.) She actually turned out to be the winner! That was great news, since individuals befriending Shabayeva would see the words "Neediest Kids." The magic of visibility.

Photo 8.4. Placement by student Nasser Romaithy.
Photo courtesy of Katherine A. Pack, Lifetime Networks—
AETN; William Swann with the Weinstein Company; Tim Gunn
and Heidi Klum with "Project Runway"; and Irina Shabeyeva,
winner of Project Runway, Season 6. Promo ad courtesy of
Lifetime Entertainment Services LLC.

Twitter represents another great opportunity in social network-ing, and again, the students used this tool to get the word out about events and activities for Neediest Kids. Students worked on a text campaign, as mentioned earlier, for people to contribute to the organization. They also used "tweeting" as a means to get others to attend several fundraising events. Again, the students tracked the number of tweets from the very beginning of the project to the end. (See Photo 8.5.)

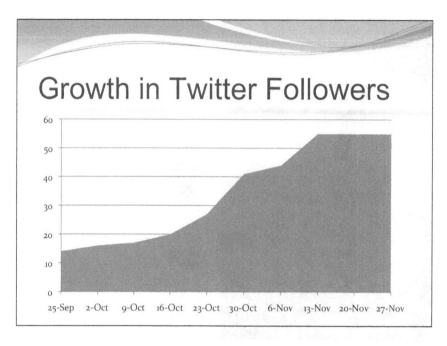

Photo 8.5. Submitted by student Natasha Carlos.

BLOGS

Blogs are extremely important for your outreach. Technorati is the site that lists the top blogs in the world. Learn who they are. Never underestimate their value in getting your client visibility. Also keep in mind that every major news organization has a blog of some sort. Major companies have realized their potential and many CEOs have their own blogs as a way to keep in contact with their consumers, stakeholders, and their employees. It is a very valuable marketing tool, and as students, you should use it as part of your strategy for your clients.

TRADITIONAL MEDIA

Regardless of what you may hear about the role of traditional media, it is still alive and well. True, the use of the Internet has revolutionized the media from where it was years ago. During Edward Bernays' time, he discussed the importance of the role of the media and the various platforms the publicist can use: "There is the moving picture; the lecture platform; there is advertising; there is the direct-by-mail effort; there is the stage-drama and music; there is word of mouth; there is the pulpit, the schoolroom, the legislative chamber..."[1] And Bernays discussed the newspaper, who "holds an important position in American life."[2] That was then. Today, newspapers may have declined but they still play an active role, as do radio and magazines. And television in its own way continues to get messages out to the public, and should be considered in your strategy. Never underestimate the value of your local newspapers, television stations, and radio stations. In the *Nothing But Nets* campaign, two students were smart enough to make a pitch to a local television station about their campus event, which was aimed at raising awareness about the use of nets that can save children's lives from malaria in Africa. The station asked the students to be on their morning program to talk about both the organization and what they were planning on campus. (See Photo 8.6.) It was a win-win situation.

---

[1] Bernays, E.L. (1923). *Crystallizing Public Opinion.* New York: Liverlight Publishing Corporation, p. 178.
[2] Ibid., p. 178.

Photo 8.6. Students Artemis Antipps and Marissa Tasho
appear with anchor Andrea Roane on WUSA-TV Channel 9,
Washington, D.C., to discuss the *Nothing But Nets* campaign.
Photo courtesy of WUSA-TV, Channel 9.

Thus, as you map out your strategy and outreach plans, remember all the elements we discussed here to make your campaign strong and effective.

9

The Midpoint: How Are Your Deliverables Coming Along?

elieve it or not, a semester can feel as if it goes by fairly quickly. Though the workload can be overwhelming, the key is to
keep on track by adhering to your well-devised PR plan and
schedule. In your PR plan, you should have created a calendar to
help you schedule client meetings, events, and outreach opportunities. You also need this calendar as a student to help guide you to
where you *should* be as the semester winds down. By the time you
get to the midpoint, you should be making progress on your deliverables. What needs to be done to get to your anticipated results?
Those results or **deliverables** are what the client wants to see.

Deliverables could include many factors, and here is a checklist
to guide you:

MARKETING MATERIALS

If you are developing new materials for your client, then that
should be the first thing you do, because you need these materials

to help with your events and outreach. You can help your client by putting your deliverables on a CD or drive that can later be given to them. All these materials will be an incredible asset for your client long after you're gone. What did you provide your client that they did not have previously? Was it a new logo? New business cards? Did you provide suggestions or additions for their annual report? Did you create new membership brochures? Were materials created for outreach to other colleges and schools in the country? Did you create posters and/or quarter sheets? Did you help compose biographies that were needed for some time? Did you create a public service announcement that they never had? Never underestimate all the work you did that shows all you have accomplished.

EVENTS

You should have scheduled a couple of events at this point. You may have one scheduled before your final presentation to your client **or** maybe there is a big event your client has asked you to spearhead or work on with them. Why is this important? Simply put, your events are the catalyst for reaching the various audiences you want. They will also be a factor in your social media and your outreach. And these events could also attract some type of media for you—be it local media or your university/college media.

SOCIAL MEDIA

What type of social media was used in your campaign? Was it getting the client's message out there? Was it strengthening what the organization does or its contributions? Was it promoting a product or service? What type of social media did you use and how many people did you reach? Can you create charts to show the number of people reached via Facebook or how many tweets were broadcasted on Twitter? Did anyone "retweet?" Did you get your message across by creating a class blog? Did you also contact other bloggers about your client? Most media outlets have a blog of some type. Did you succeed in getting your client in any of these?

TRADITIONAL MEDIA

Did you succeed in getting any print interviews, television interviews, or radio mentions for your organization or client? What you may not realize is that your involvement with your client may generate media attention for your college or university as well. That is a win-win situation for you. Traditional media is very important and your client knows it. Don't neglect these outlets and think that it's impossible. Be positive and see where this can all lead. (Example: Several years ago, my students worked with Franco Nuschese, a brilliant restaurateur in Washington, D.C. The students helped with the publicity of a second restaurant Nuschese was opening in Virginia. One particular student worked on securing local media. She called a television station, which asked the chef to come along with Nuschese for a demonstration of a new item on their menu. That was great news! Even greater news: the anchor also wanted the student to be interviewed on camera to discuss the class project! It was a great opportunity for both our university and the entrepreneur!)

SURVEYS/STUDIES

Did you conduct some type of study or survey to help your client? This is monumental. The results are essential for your client to assess their business model and are worth a thousand words. They make wonderful deliverables.

COMMUNICATION AUDIT

Providing an assessment of how the company or organization is doing is vital. An audit is a valuable piece of information for your client and basically gives them a picture of how the company is doing and what others think of them. This is a lengthy process, but the results are priceless.

Once again, these are important ideas for you to consider as you prepare for your final presentation, which will be discussed in the next chapter.

10

The Final Presentation: Your Hard Work Comes Together

This is it. The big moment has arrived—the final presentation. Are you prepared? Here is the challenge: There is a tendency once the semester is in full swing to just "ride the tide." It happens to all of us, but don't be complacent. It's time for you to show off all the great work you've done. Set goals for your client as well as for yourself. In real life, there may be cases where you do not have the luxury of working with a client for 15 plus weeks. That is a long stretch of time. Thus, you must prepare yourself, as mentioned in the earlier chapters, so you are ready to go on with the final presentation. In Chapter 11, I will provide examples of presentations. But first, let me explain how it all comes together.

Gearing up for the final presentation is a daunting task and there are several ways to approach it. I have categorized these into two areas. One involves the elements needed for your presentation. The second explains how you should prepare for the actual day you are presenting.

ELEMENTS OF THE PRESENTATION

Teamwork

As mentioned in Chapter 6, "Teamwork," there should be groups assigned to various tasks or responsibilities. Each team should have a leader or co-leader(s) who assembles weekly reports for the client. Each individual in the group is accountable for what they have contributed to the project. For example, if you helped to develop **marketing materials**, then you should include those in either a PowerPoint presentation or other visual presentation. Again, some of these materials can include a new brochure, a new logo, or perhaps even new biographies. And you should also have copies of these materials on a CD to hand to your client at the end of the presentation. Remember, you are leaving a legacy.

If you handled the **media** on the team, you should include a press list or table listing the media outlet, the individual contacted, and their phone number and e-mail address. Media can be separated according to whether they are national, local, print, broadcast, or internet outlets. You must also let your client know the response you received. Remember, it takes a great deal of time to contact the media, and though you may have only succeeded with a few placements, if that, you must demonstrate to the client all the time and effort involved.

If you were responsible for **events** on your team, you must show and mention the events, your outreach, the attendees, and the results. Showing photographs or images are vital. You can also include the promotional materials that you used to attract individuals to your event(s). The greatest part of your events presentation is showing your client the money you raised, if possible. That is always a wonderful and surprising element for them and you can be sure that they will be grateful.

If you handled **outreach**, specifically social networking, and there is a great story to tell, be sure to provide examples. Did you take the client's Facebook fan page from just a few members to hundreds? Did you tweet from the beginning of the semester up until hours before your presentation? What did you tweet, and were you able to track the tweets? Did you make major changes on their website? Show those changes and the number of people that have come to the new site to see and hear about the client.

Estimated Costs and Impressions

As you get closer to the end of the presentation, document the number of people you have reached via social media, the number of impressions from your media, and the money you have raised. One of your last slides should include the number of hours you have spent on the project. For example, you should calculate the hours you worked on the project each week. What is the going rate for someone starting at a PR firm? These all vary.

According to a 2010 Salary Survey by *PR Week*, the average salary for an account coordinator is $29,897.[1] That's the yearly salary. So let's say hypothetically, you would bill about $75.00 an hour. (This is just an example.) You would then add up the total hours you worked individually per week. For example, if it's 5 hours per week, multiply that by $75.00. Your total billing for a week is around $375. If you have worked 15 weeks, multiply 15 by $375. The total you could have billed the client is $5,625. If there are 20 students in the class, take the $5,625 and multiply that by 20. That total is $112,500 and that is the bill you would have presented to the client if they had to pay you as a class. That is an important aspect of your class and presentation. You are giving the client a clear picture of what your time is worth.

However, that does not include the number of impressions (people who have heard, seen, or read about your client or message) generated. You must calculate the number of impressions overall for the client. As PR practitioners, we know the value of these metrics and how they would translate into advertising dollars. Your client received this value free of charge so you must make them realize that as young professionals, you achieved a great deal.

---

[1] www.prweekus.com. (2010, March, p. 30.) Retrieved on June 10, 2010 from www.prweekus.com.

Again, these are some important things that you should prepare as you get ready for the final day. With that said, let's move on to that final day.

THE BIG DAY—THE ACTUAL PRESENTATION

How you present your work to the client may certainly vary. You can visit them at their office or have them come to you. My recommendation is to welcome them to your university or college. One suggestion is to possibly provide a reception for the client and select a nice classroom or small theater to deliver your visual presentation. This reception should not be elaborate by any means. It could be something as simple as tea and crackers, chips and lemonade, or coffee and donuts. It is a great way of mingling with your client later and hearing feedback. The event should generally take place at the same time the class is held. *This is an important factor to remember.* Before the semester begins and you are selecting your client, it is imperative for you to request that they be at that presentation. It is the least they can do since you are providing a great deal of work and exposure for them.

As you prepare for that day, you may also want to send personal invitations to your client. You can send them via Evites, but I have found that clients love receiving them through snail mail. Delivering physical media also shows your ability to put together a nice event with beautiful materials. Make certain you include an RSVP and then follow up with a phone call. Include directions as well as parking information if other members of the organization attend. For example, in one case, we had members of a board attend a presentation, and they were thrilled to be invited—but they needed information on how to get to the university, including parking.

You must also prepare the type of food you want, as well as a theme for your small reception. Do you want to color-coordinate the reception area with the colors of your organization/client? Do you want to create posters and place them on easels to promote your event throughout the campus and your department? These posters also serve a tool in directing your guests to the location of the presentation. What will you wear as students? Is it business casual? Again, is there a theme for your client? In one case, students wore black and red to symbolize an organization and they ordered bracelets in orange and yellow to hand out to the guests supporting their cause.

Should you have a program? What should the program include? If you choose to do one, make certain that several students greet the guests with the program as they walk into the presentation. In terms of content, whom should you thank in the program? Local businesses, the community, your university, your dean, etc.? All these little touches make a presentation special and worth remembering.

Should you give your client a token of appreciation for the semester? Could it be a photo of the class in a frame? Could it be something in your university or college bookstore that would remind the client about you and the class? Perhaps a mug, a pillow, a sweatshirt, a book? Again, all these add up to creating a special and memorable presentation. And as you end that presentation, all of your work throughout the past 15 weeks will reaffirm the commitment and passion you've demonstrated. You will long remember that day and the contributions you've made.

Congratulations! You have achieved the perfect PR portfolio. Now it's on to the big "real world." Godspeed!

Case Studies

Examples of students' works:

PROJECT: "HOMEFRONT: STORIES OF AMERICA AT WAR"

Explanation: Public Communication students were asked to work with their colleagues from the Journalism Division, who were putting together a film about men and women returning from the war overseas. The project was spearheaded by Professor Rick Rockwell. Students in the Portfolio class were asked to promote the documentary, which aired on the MHz Networks. Photos 11.1 to 11.4 include a few items from the class and presentation.

Photo 11.1

Photo 11.2. Poster image created by student Brendan Steidle.
Concept created by student Erika Eckstrom.

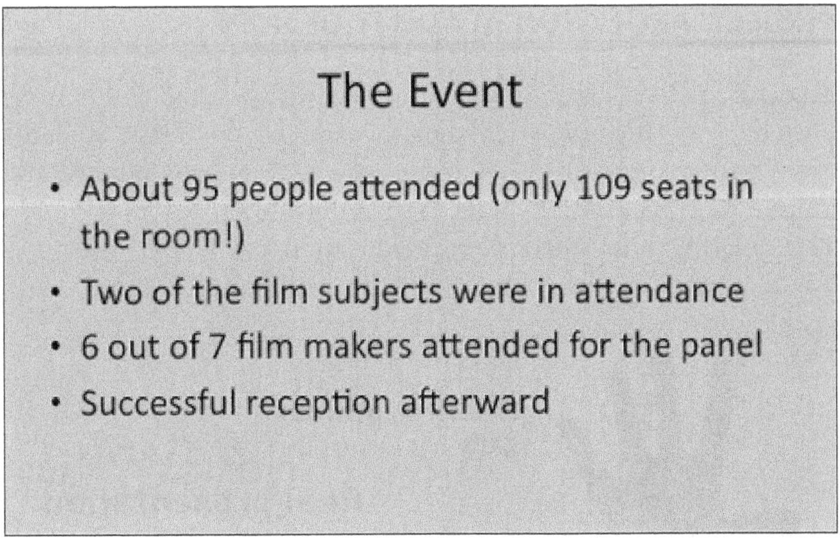

The Event
About 95 people attended (only 109 seats in the room!)
Two of the film subjects were in attendance
6 out of 7 film makers attended for the panel
Successful reception afterward

Photo 11.3

Homefront: Stories of America at War

The raw emotion of war is experienced not only by warriors on the battle ...

... the Weschler Theatre. "The students are the ones who did the heavy lifting here. They're ... has to do the job to bring it forward."

Homefront accomplishes that. Time and again through stellar reporting and interviewing, the students get to the core of their subjects' beliefs, pains, fears, and hopes. Consider these stirring moments in the program:

"It's heartbreaking, sometimes, to see my family," says Joe Young, a serviceman on a two week leave from Iraq. The pressure to enjoy every minute of this precious time with his loved ones in tiny Windber, Penn., can in a different way be as stressful as combat.

"In my mind, my chaplain will come home before me," says Pfc. William H. Bolling, a chaplain's assistant dedicated to ensuring the safety of the chaplain he guards—even at the ultimate cost.

"It's like I can never come home," says Vaughan Wilson, a paratrooper suffering from PTSD. "The war will never leave me, I will never leave the war."

Glenn Luther served as associate producer of the special, and also produced a segment about the global news network Al Jazeera English. He had only two hours of access to the network's Washington bureau chief and a key reporter.

"It really taught you that you have to be on the edge of your seat ready to go," he says of the reporting experience. "You only have two hours, so if you're not [ready], you could miss the story. I'm very proud of the product we put out. This is exactly what I want to do as a journalist."

Mission truly accomplished.

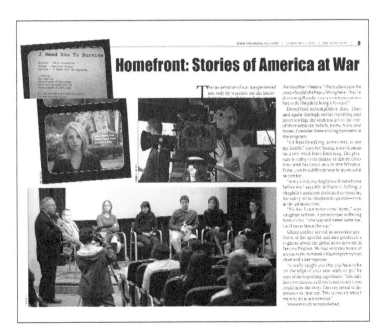

Photo 11.4. Photo of American University Professor Rick Rockwell with several of the students from the "Homefront" project. Courtesy of *American Today*. Students involved with the project include: Jennifer Tyre, Elizabeth Mendes, Brittany Keil, Michael Wargo, Cara Schayer, Mariam Simpson, Glenn Luther, and Ann Keil.

PROJECT: ARLINGTON ACADEMY OF HOPE

Students helped this local nonprofit, which aids children in Uganda with education and health care. In this class, students raised the awareness of AAH at the university and community, and helped the organization plan their annual gala. Photos 11.5 to 11.36 highlight aspects of their presentation.

Photo 11.5

Welcome

- PR Portfolio Group: The class and objectives
- Marketing materials
- Outreach
- Media
- Events
- Looking Ahead: The SanGala
- In the end...
- Thank you

Photo 11.6

Do you want the perfect job after graduation?

One way to get there is to register for the
PR Portfolio Group class!
COMM 496, Wed. 2:10-4:50 pm
This course will involve all aspects of a PR campaign including media placements, social marketing, planning events, using marketing tools, and more. You'll build a professional portfolio that's comparable to any boutique firm in the industry.
Sound exciting? Space is limited, register soon!

Course Requirements:
GPA of 3.6 or higher
Students must receive an A- in both COMM 337 (PR Writing) and COMM 301 (Public Relations)
Permission from your academic advisor
Contact Prof. Gemma Puglisi with questions

This year's client is the **Arlington Academy of Hope** which is a volunteer, non-profit organization based in the United States that helps children in rural Uganda reach their full potential.
www.arlingtonacademyofhope.org

Photo 11.7. Poster created by graduate student Allison Lane.

Objectives

Increase Visibility	Raise Funds	Leave a Legacy
• Getting the word out • College students • Media • Potential volunteers	• Bar events • Quad event • Pitch letters • Bracelets	• Media lists • Local organizations • Targeted outreach • Materials for AAH

Photo 11.8

Marketing Materials

Photo 11.9

ARLINGTON ACADEMY OF HOPE

get involved

You're a college student. You want to help, but you're broke, busy, and you really want to go out Friday night. Here are some easy ways to still get involved:

1 DONATE

- Donate on your own, donate with friends... any amount helps!
- Go to our website to donate quickly and easily, or mail a check the old-fashioned way.

2 VOLUNTEER

- Looking for a resume boost, community service project or summer plans? AAH has plenty of opportunities both in DC and abroad!
- Help AAH spread the word in DC and around the US
- Travel to Uganda for a chance to volunteer directly with AAH and work with Ugandan students, a life-changing experience!

3 GET THE HOOK UP

- Sign up for our email list, become an AAH fan and/or friend on Facebook, or follow us on Twitter @AAHUganda. You follow us, we'll follow you!

4 SPONSOR A CHILD

- Roommates? Sports Teams? Clubs? Greek life? Get together and sponsor a student in Uganda. For just $300, send a child to AAH for a whole year with everything they need. Make it an annual tradition and see them succeed through all of school!

5 HOLD A FUNDRAISER

- Got a friend of a friend who's a bartender? See if they will sponsor a fundraiser for AAH! Who needs to leave home? Throw a party and charge $5 at the door! Who doesn't love cupcakes? Hold a bake sale on your quad! Get your friends in on helping AAH and really make a difference.

6 TWEET, TEXT, TELL

- Spread the word about AAH to friends, family, professors and your Facebook and Twitter followers.

For more about how to help, visit the AAH website or email **info@AAHUganda.org**

P.O. Box 7694 - Arlington, VA 22207 - 703.201.2483 - **www.ArlingtonAcademyofHope.org**

Photo 11.10

ARLINGTON ACADEMY OF

HOPE

How to host a screening of
From One Village: A Story of Hope in Uganda
AAH's 20-minute film

host a screening

Why host a screening?

Hosting an informal screening of *From One Village* for peers, colleagues, a civic group, school or place of worship is a great way to spread the word about the plight of children in Uganda and the difference the Arlington Academy of Hope is making. Just follow these six easy steps.

1 Think through logistics and invite your guests.

Who will you invite? Where and when will you hold your screening? Send out emails to get the ball rolling. See our website for sample email invitations.

2 Tell us about your event!

Contact us 10-14 days before your event so we can send you the *From One Village* DVD and AAH brochures. Please let us know when you will hold your screening, the organization or group that you're hosting it for, how many people you expect and your mailing address and phone number. (Note: you can also stream the documentary from the AAH website rather than use the DVD.)

3 Learn about AAH's programs and background info.

Read the AAH fact sheet for a quick overview of the organization and Uganda or check out the AAH website.

4 Use the AAH talking points provided.

The talking points sheet includes suggested remarks for before and after showing the film, as well as what to say to the audience members who ask how they can help.

5 Have the following materials available for audience members:

- AAH brochures
- Get Involved handout
- Child sponsorship program overview and child sponsorship application
- Sign-up sheet for AAH email list
- AAH website URL:
  www.ArlingtonAcademyofHope.org

6 Tell us how it went.

We'd love to hear how your screening went! Please email us at:

info@AAHUganda.org

or send sign-up sheets for our email list to:

Arlington Academy of Hope
PO Box 7694
Arlington, VA 22207

For more about hosting a screening, please visit the AAH website.

P.O. Box 7694 - Arlington, VA 22207 - 703.201.2483 - www.ArlingtonAcademyofHope.org

Photo 11.11

ARLINGTON ACADEMY OF

HOPE

What to say when you are hosting a screening of
From One Village: A Story of Hope in Rural Uganda

talking points

Give background information about AAH

- The Arlington Academy of Hope is a nonprofit organization founded in 2004 in Arlington, VA by two Ugandan immigrants named John and Joyce Wanda. They grew up in remote villages in one of the most impoverished areas of Eastern Uganda and against all odds, eventually earned college degrees and immigrated to the US in 1996 through a State Department visa lottery program.

- In 2004 they founded AAH and opened a primary school, also called the Arlington Academy of Hope, in John's native village in Uganda. The organization has evolved to offer secondary school scholarships, healthcare and community development in addition to one of the most competitive primary schools in Uganda.

- AAH serves as a beacon of hope for children and their communities in rural Uganda who are in a constant struggle against hunger and disease and lack electricity, running water, healthcare and education.

Introduce the film

- This documentary, entitled *From One Village: A Story of Hope in Rural Uganda*, shows what life is like for 3 young people and how the availability of educational opportunities shape their lives.

Show the film

- Either play the DVD or stream the documentary directly from the AAH website.

Post-screening remarks

- The poor quality of the public education system in Uganda has led many families to decide that their children would be better off working the fields than in schools with unqualified teachers and few textbooks.

- Children who do attend find it difficult to learn.

Post-screening remarks (cont.)

- Only 14% of students across Uganda, with far less in rural areas, continue to secondary school.

- Today, AAH is regarded as a model primary school throughout Uganda. For four consecutive years 100% of AAH graduates have passed the national standardized exams and nearly all have gone on to secondary school.

- AAH's other programs include two rural health clinics, a library, economic development efforts and outreach to 13 local village schools.

Invite the audience to get involved

- What you've seen in this film – the transformational power of education and the chance to seek a better life – is possible because of the generosity of people like you and me.

- AAH strives to reach more children and expand their programs from one village to another.

Provide ways to get involved with AAH

- Sponsor a child

- Make a donation

- Volunteer in the US or Uganda

- Host your own screening of *From One Village* or share the online video of the documentary

- Introduce AAH to individuals or organizations who would be interested in helping

- Sign up for AAH's e-newsletter (pass around a sign-up sheet and later mail or email it to AAH)

- Join AAH on Facebook or follow us on Twitter

Discuss the AAH website

- Write the URL for all to see or spell it out.

- Visit the AAH website to watch the film again, or to learn more about AAH programs and how you can help.

P.O. Box 7694 - Arlington, VA 22207 - 703.201.2483 - www.ArlingtonAcademyofHope.org

Photo 11.12

ARLINGTON ACADEMY OF

HOPE **stay in touch**

Sign up for the AAH email list to stay in touch! On Facebook? Do you tweet? Become an AAH friend or follow us on Twitter.

NAME	E-MAIL ADDRESS

Either mail this sheet to the address below, or email to info@AAHUganda.org—or you can always sign up directly through the AAH website.

P.O. Box 7694 - Arlington, VA 22207 - 703.201.2483 - www.ArlingtonAcademyofHope.org

Photo 11.13

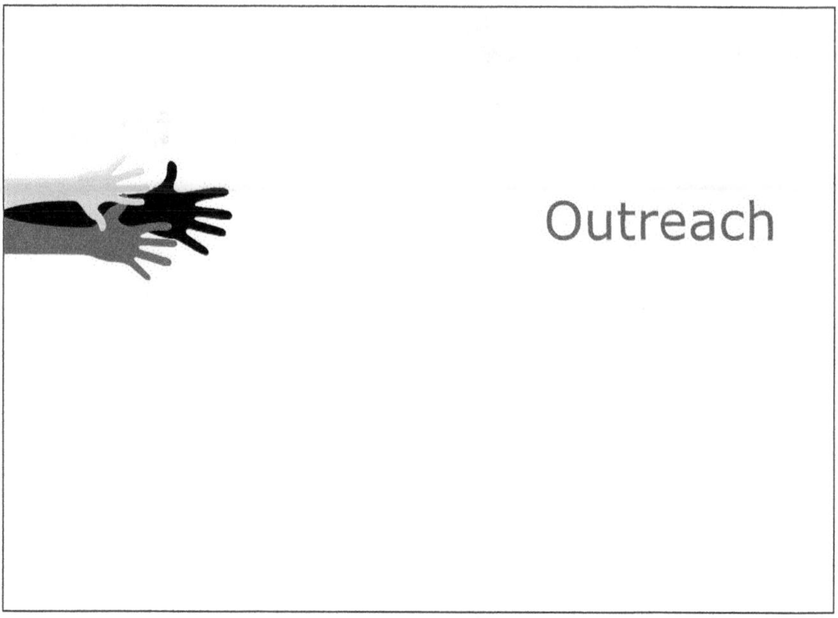

Outreach

Photo 11.14

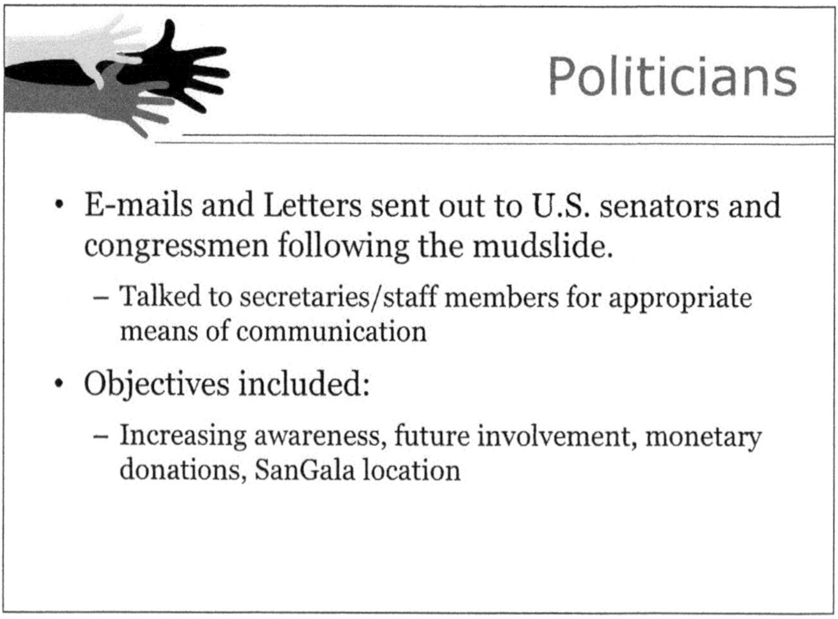

Politicians

- E-mails and Letters sent out to U.S. senators and congressmen following the mudslide.
  - Talked to secretaries/staff members for appropriate means of communication
- Objectives included:
  - Increasing awareness, future involvement, monetary donations, SanGala location

Photo 11.15

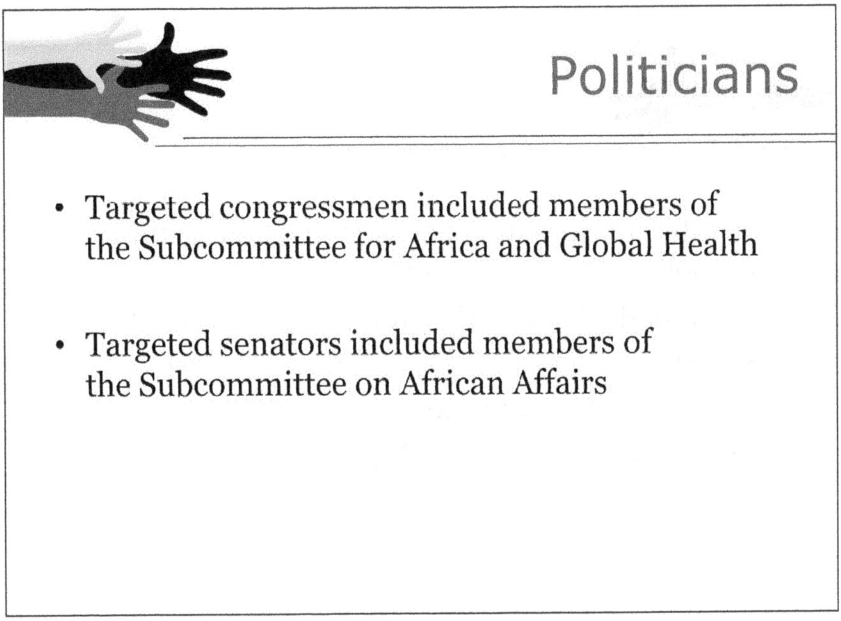

Politicians

- Targeted congressmen included members of the Subcommittee for Africa and Global Health

- Targeted senators included members of the Subcommittee on African Affairs

Photo 11.16

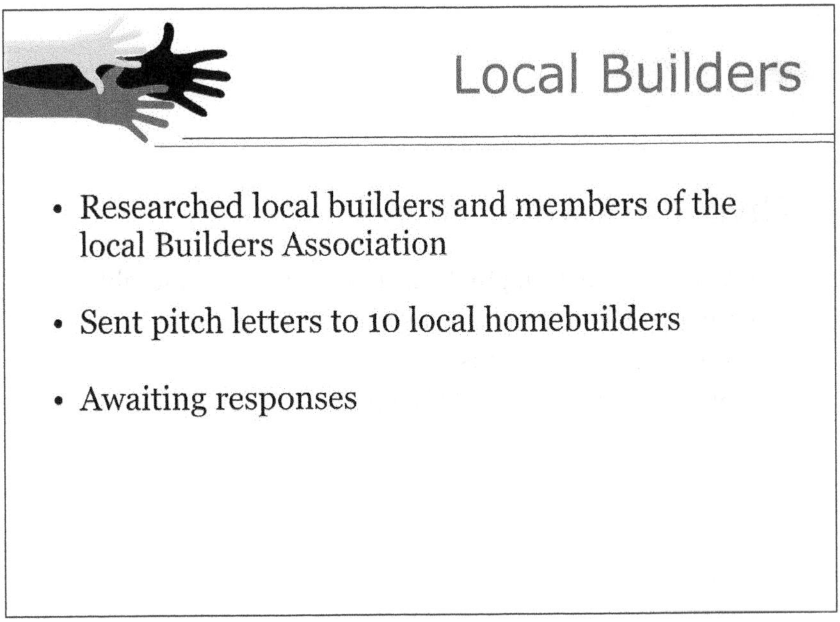

Local Builders

- Researched local builders and members of the local Builders Association

- Sent pitch letters to 10 local homebuilders

- Awaiting responses

Photo 11.17

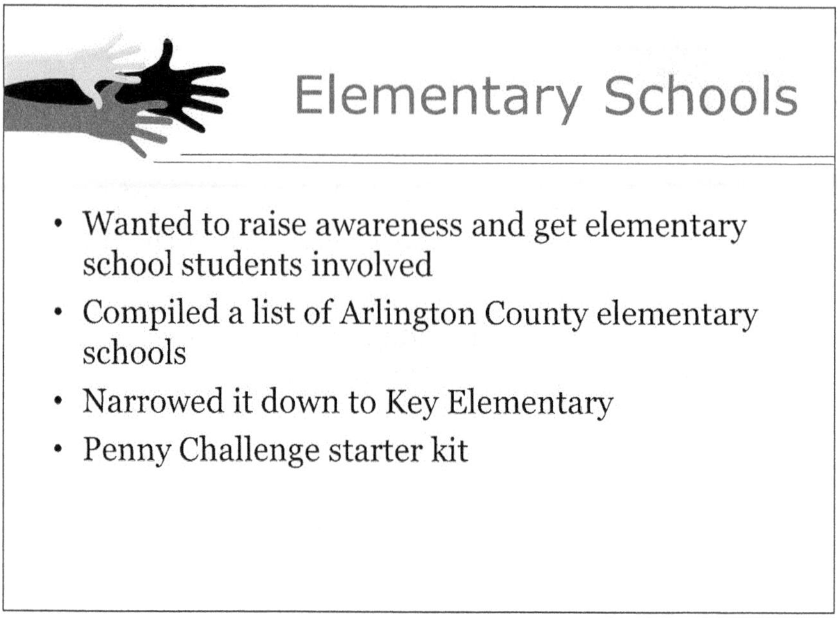

Elementary Schools

- Wanted to raise awareness and get elementary school students involved
- Compiled a list of Arlington County elementary schools
- Narrowed it down to Key Elementary
- Penny Challenge starter kit

Photo 11.18

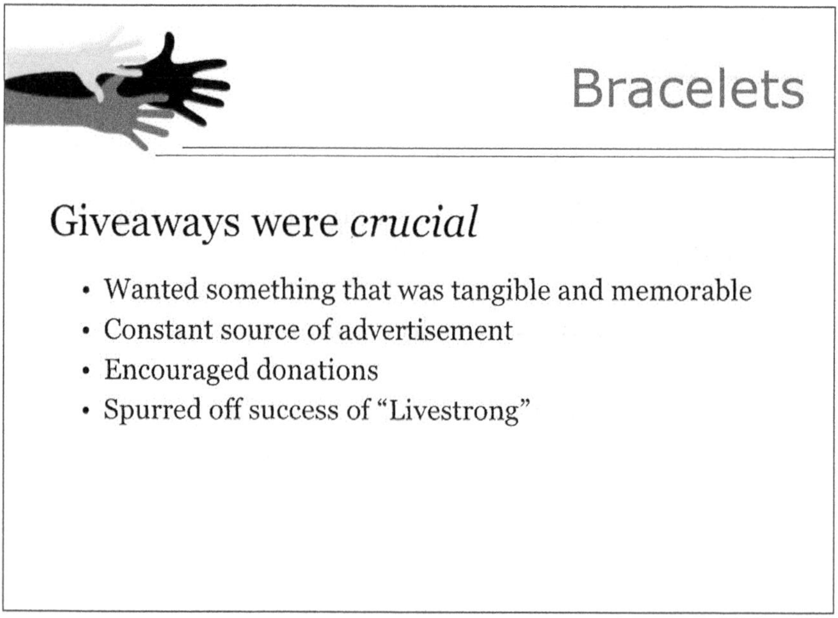

Bracelets

Giveaways were *crucial*

- Wanted something that was tangible and memorable
- Constant source of advertisement
- Encouraged donations
- Spurred off success of "Livestrong"

Photo 11.19

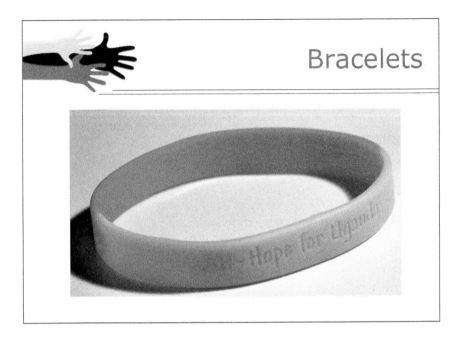

Photo 11.20

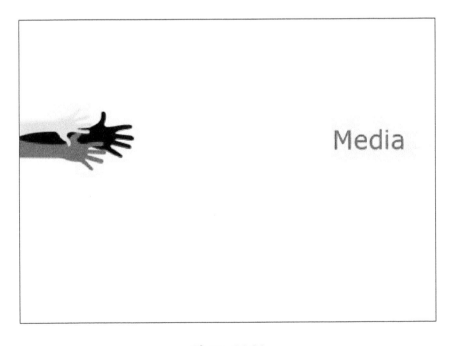

Photo 11.21

Media Relations

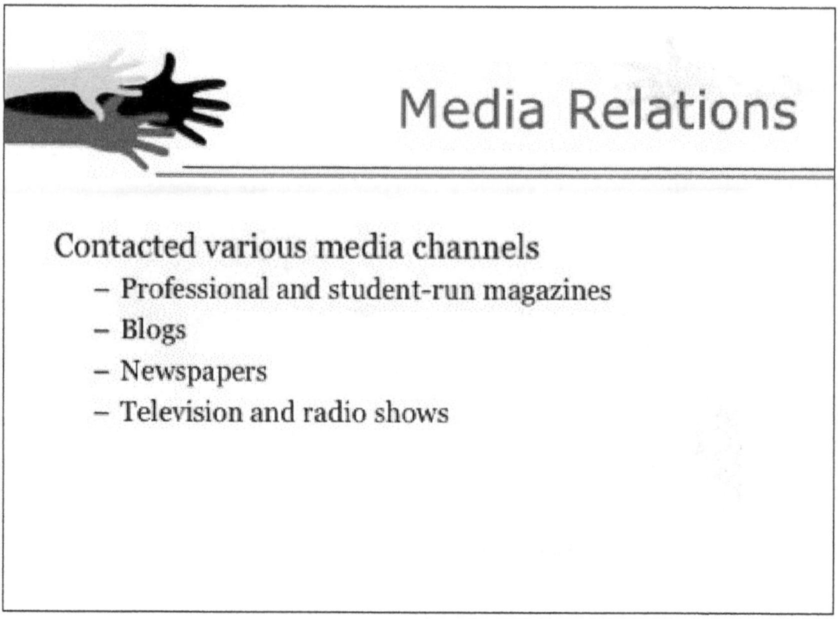

Contacted various media channels
- Professional and student-run magazines
- Blogs
- Newspapers
- Television and radio shows

Photo 11.22

Events

Photo 11.23

Panel Discussion

Tues. March 30 – AU's Mary Graydon Center – 8:30 pm

Sustainable Development:
The Many Facets of Community Empowerment

Panelists:
- **John Wanda,** founder of the Arlington Academy of Hope
- **Nicole Hewitt,** Program Officer at the Institute for Sustainable Communities
- **Andrea Bachmann**, American University student returned from Alternative Break in Colombia

Photo 11.24

Photo 11.25. Photo permission granted by the Arlington Academy of Hope.

Outcomes

- Event posted on Brightest Young Things blog
- Over 100 attendees
- Total amount raised:

$541

Photo 11.26

Recess for Hope

Wed. April 7 – AU Quad – 2 to 5 pm

- Recess-style games
- Ice cream fundraiser
- Bracelet sale
- Sponsorship from Honest Tea
- Posted 50 fliers and door-hangers on AU campus
- Contacted *The Eagle* and ATV

Photo 11.27

Photo 11.28

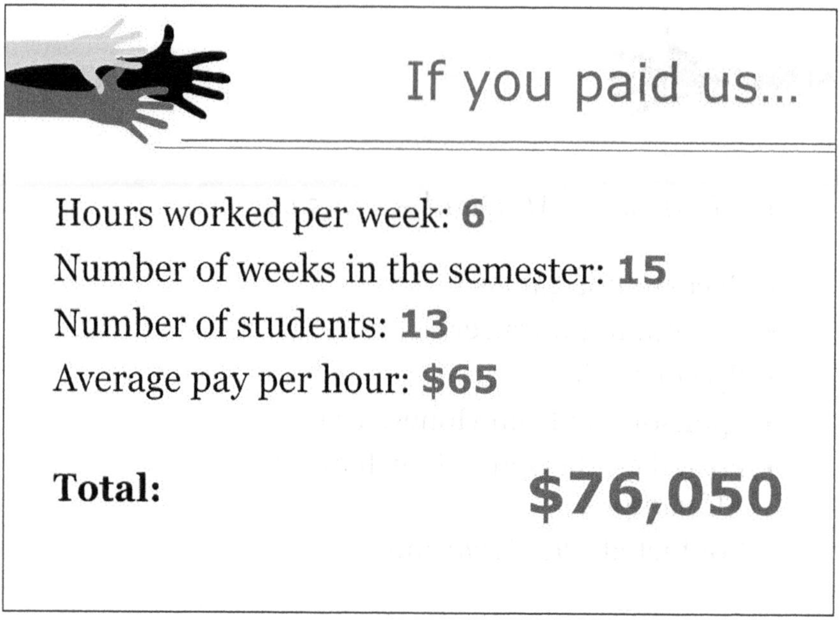

If you paid us...

Hours worked per week: **6**

Number of weeks in the semester: **15**

Number of students: **13**

Average pay per hour: **$65**

Total: **$76,050**

Photo 11.29

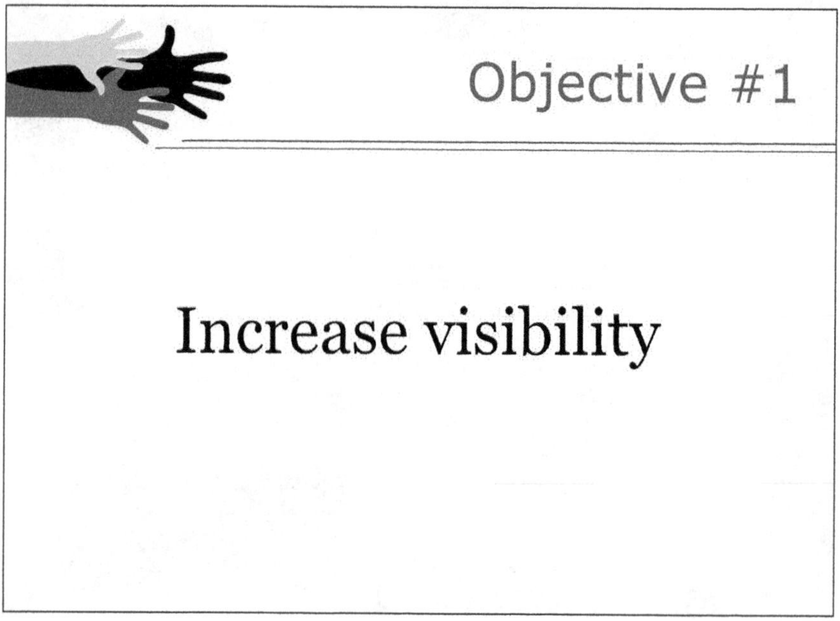

Objective #1

Increase visibility

Photo 11.30

Media: Impressions

AU campus media *The Eagle* (print and online) and ATV	16,000+
Blogs The Arlington Academy of Hope Brightest Young Things The Sweetest Thing—DC A Local Foodie's Fight Hey Jess	1,000+
Social Media Facebook and Twitter	4,000+
Total:	**21,000+**

Photo 11.31

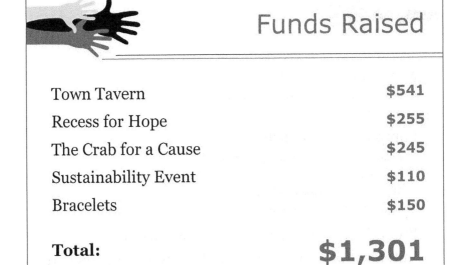

Funds Raised

Town Tavern	$541
Recess for Hope	$255
The Crab for a Cause	$245
Sustainability Event	$110
Bracelets	$150
Total:	**$1,301**

Photo 11.32

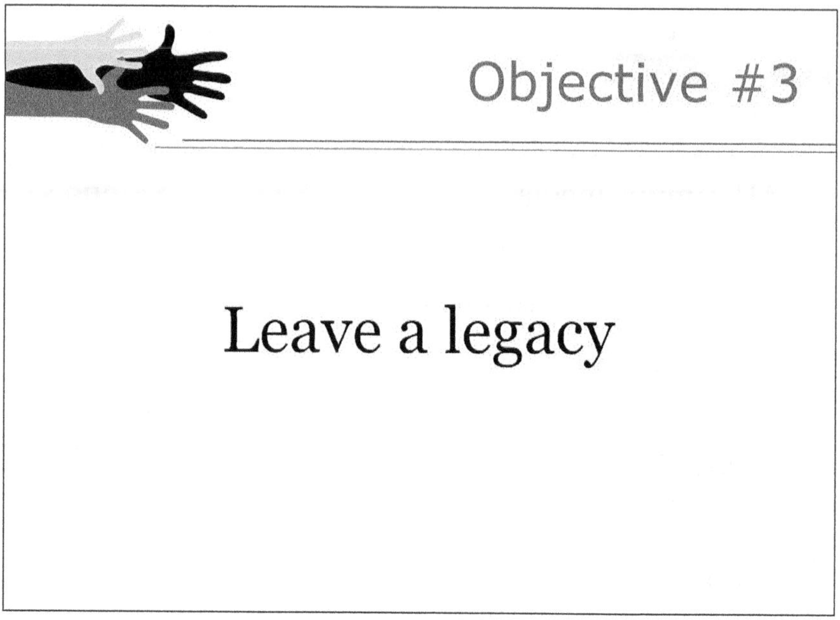

Objective #3

Leave a legacy

Photo 11.33

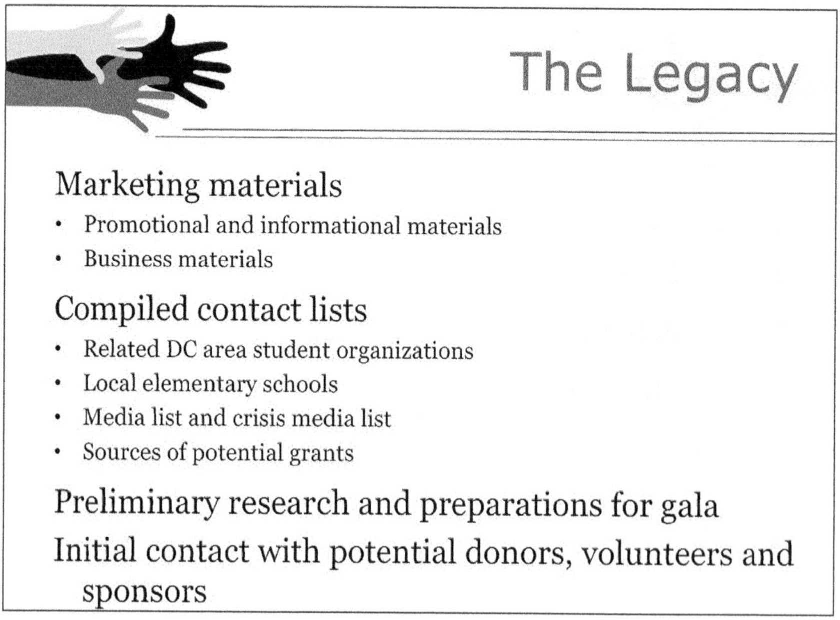

The Legacy

Marketing materials
- Promotional and informational materials
- Business materials

Compiled contact lists
- Related DC area student organizations
- Local elementary schools
- Media list and crisis media list
- Sources of potential grants

Preliminary research and preparations for gala

Initial contact with potential donors, volunteers and sponsors

Photo 11.34

Recommendations

- Have marketing materials available for download on website
- Utilize target promotional packets and professionally printed business cards
- Follow up with interested schools for penny challenge
  - Make it annual: the school can continue to sponsor the same child!
- Follow up with medical students interested in volunteering
- Maintain contact with related college student organizations
  - To get further involved in Africa, sustainable development, and healthcare, and education issues on college campuses.

Photo 11.35

Recommendations

- Increase use of social media and pitches to blogs
  - Check out social media just for nonprofits (ie. Care2.com)
- Think about making a kid-friendly teaser video
  - To go viral on the web or use for penny challenge
- Host occasional bar or restaurant fundraisers, small events
- Distribute or sell bracelets through website and at events
- Aim big with the gala!
  - Try a celebrity or political guest to instantly boost attendance

Photo 11.36

PROJECT: PUBLIC COMMUNICATION PRACTICUM PROJECT

Rebuilding a website for "Figs Fine Foods"—a café in Washington, D.C. (Graduate Students: Esra Alhabib and Leila Sidawy.) This class is the graduate version of the PR Portfolio. Students were asked to "find" a client and help them with their needs, including PR, media, a web component, and marketing tools. Two students took on the challenge to rebuild this café's website. Photos 11.37 to 11.64 illustrate the steps of their process and the results they achieved.

Photo 11.37

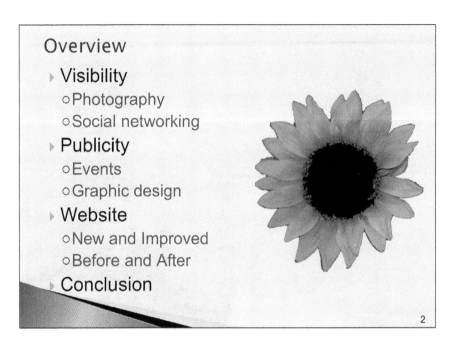

Photo 11.38

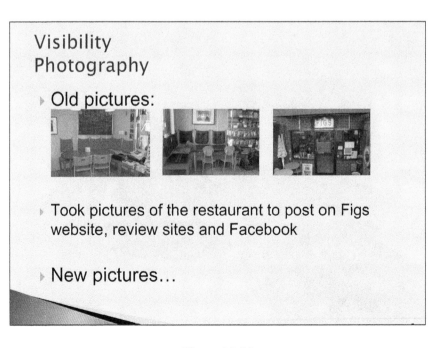

Photo 11.39

Photo 11.40

Photo 11.41

Photo 11.42

Photo 11.43

Photo 11.44

Photo 11.45

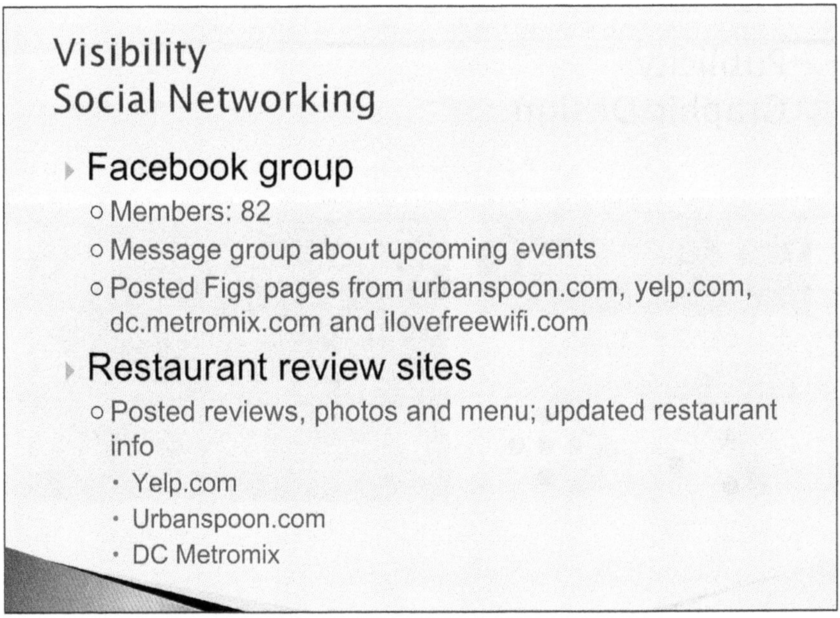

Visibility
Social Networking

▸ Facebook group
  ○ Members: 82
  ○ Message group about upcoming events
  ○ Posted Figs pages from urbanspoon.com, yelp.com, dc.metromix.com and ilovefreewifi.com

▸ Restaurant review sites
  ○ Posted reviews, photos and menu; updated restaurant info
    · Yelp.com
    · Urbanspoon.com
    · DC Metromix

Photo 11.46

Publicity
Events

▸ SOC Game Night
  ○ Wednesday, February 18th
  ○ Created Facebook event page
  ○ Created and distributed digital invitation

▸ Cooking Class
  ○ Wednesday, March 25th
  ○ Created and distributed digital invitation
  ○ Sent Facebook message to group members

Photo 11.47

Photo 11.48

Photo 11.49

Publicity
Graphic Design

Photo 11.50

Publicity
Graphic Design

Photo 11.51

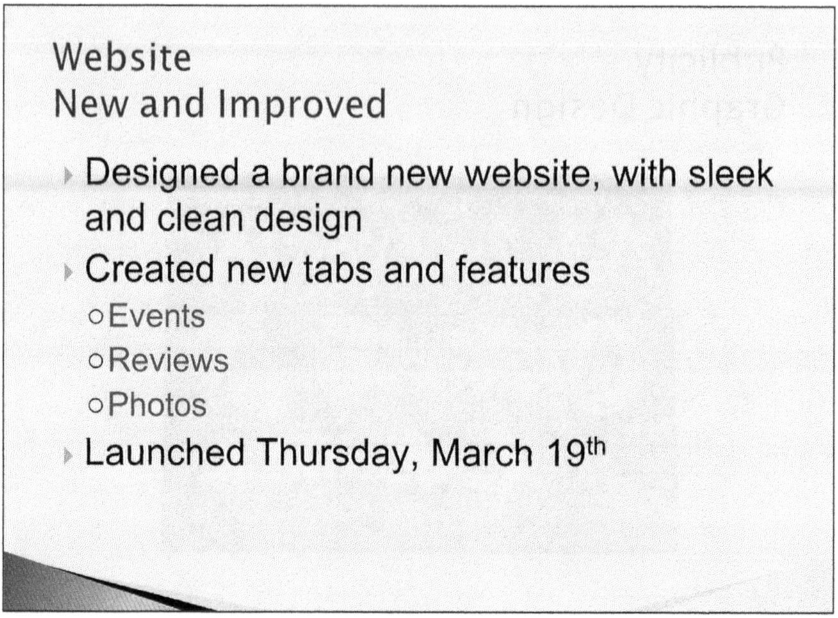

Website
New and Improved

▸ Designed a brand new website, with sleek and clean design
▸ Created new tabs and features
  ○ Events
  ○ Reviews
  ○ Photos
▸ Launched Thursday, March 19th

Photo 11.52

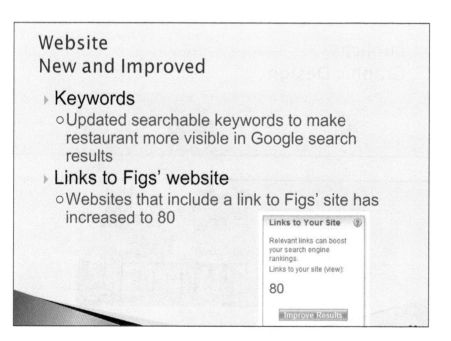

Website
New and Improved

▸ Keywords
  ○ Updated searchable keywords to make restaurant more visible in Google search results
▸ Links to Figs' website
  ○ Websites that include a link to Figs' site has increased to 80

Links to Your Site

Relevant links can boost your search engine rankings.
Links to your site (view):

80

Improve Results

Photo 11.53

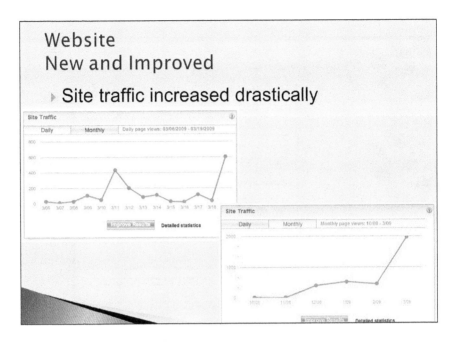

Photo 11.54

Photo 11.55

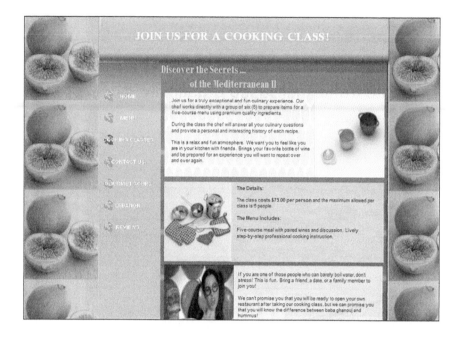

Photo 11.56

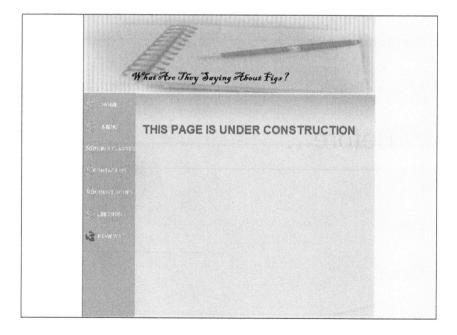

Photo 11.57

Photo 11.58

Photo 11.59

Photo 11.60

Photo 11.61

Photo 11.62

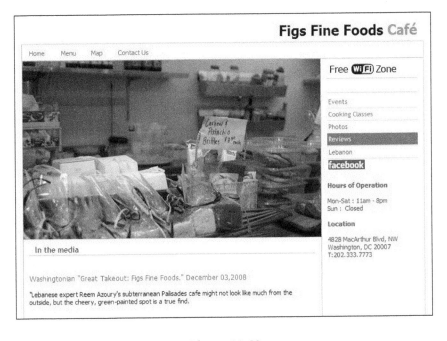

Photo 11.63

Photo 11.64